TABLE OF CONTENTS

LOS ANGELES RAMS

ACROSS

1. Offensive tackle from LSD (2017-2020) who had been a 2nd round pick by the Bengals (2006-2016) and has made 4 Pro Bowls to date, one with the Rams (2017). He has made 220 NFL starts, including 56 with Los Angeles. He wears #77.

3. First name of the player referred to in 9 ACROSS.

4. Receiver from Eastern Washington (2017-2020) who was a 2nd round pick by the Rams. To date, he has had 2 seasons with 90+ catches (2019 & 2020) and one with 1,000 receiving yards (2019). In 2019 he also had a career-best 10 touchdown catches. He has worn #18 & #10.

5. Head coach (2012-2016) whose Ram teams went just 31-45-1 and never had a winning season. He was fired late in the team's first year in Los Angeles. As head coach of the Oilers/Titans (1994-2010), he went 142-120 with one Super Bowl appearance (a loss to the Rams in 2000).

7. First name of the player referred to in 8 DOWN.

8. Real estate billionaire from St. Louis who became full owner of the Rams in 2010 and moved the team back to Los Angeles. He is responsible for the construction of the team's palatial, new stadium.

12. Ram head coach (2017-2020) who took the job at age 30 and became the youngest head coach in modern NFL history. He has not had a losing season and his teams have gone 43-21 with one Super Bowl appearance. He is regarded as one of the brightest offensive minds in the league.

13. The franchise began life in 1936 as the _____ Rams.

16. Kicker from Nebraska-Omaha and Missouri Western (2012-2019) who was a 6th round pick by the Rams and a 2017 Pro Bowler. His 201 career field goals are #2 in franchise history and his 38 field goals in 2017 led the NFL. He moved on to Dallas for 2020. He wore #4.

17. First name of the player referred to in 2 ACROSS.

19. The 2017 Rams were beaten by the _____ in a Wild Card game by a score of 26- 13.

21. The 2018 Rams were beaten by the _____ in the Super Bowl by a score of 13-3.

22. Defensive tackle from Pittsburgh (2014-2020) who was a 1st round pick by the Rams. He is a 7-time Pro Bowler and a 3-time NFL Defensive Player of the Year. He led the NFL in sacks in 2018 and is a member of the NFL 2010s All-Decade Team. He wears #99.

23. Running back from Florida State (2020) who was a 2nd round pick by the Rams and led the team with 625 rushing yards as a rookie. He also had 221 rushing yards in the team's two playoff games. He wears #23.

25. The first name of the player referred to in 7 ACROSS.

29. Defensive back from Washington (2018-2019) who had been a 1st round pick by the Chiefs (2015-2017). He was dealt to the Ravens in mid-season 2019 and played with Baltimore in 2020. He helped the 2018 Rams reach the Super Bowl and was a 2019 Pro Bowler. He wore #22.

31. Receiver from Oregon State (20180-2019) who had been a 1st round pick by the Saints (2014-2016). He was with the Patriots in 2017 and spent 2020 with the Texans. To date, he has five 1,000 receiving yard seasons including 1,204 yards for the Rams in 2018. He wore #12.

35. Tight end from Western Kentucky (2016-2020) who was a 4th round pick by the Rams. He has appeared in 78 out of a possible 80 games with the Rams and made 69 starts. He has caught

173 passes to date, with a career-high 69 in 2019. He wears #89.

37. The new stadium in which the Rams play their home games is located in _____.

38. Quarterback from Georgia (2021) who had been taken 1st overall by the Lions, for whom he had 45,000 passing yards. Despite these numbers, his under-talented Detroit teams went just 74-90. Great things are expected of him with the Rams in 2021. He wore #9.

40. Interim Ram head coach who took over when the coach referred to in 5 ACROSS was fired after 13 games in 2016. He went 0-3 to finish the season and was not retained. His recently-deceased dad led the 2000 Giants to an appearance in the Super Bowl.

41. The Rams came to Los Angeles for the first time in nineteen-forty-_____.

42. When the Rams returned to Los Angeles in 2016, they played their home games in the _____.

43. The first name of the player referred to in 9 DOWN.

44. On their way to the Super Bowl, the 2018 Rams beat _____ in a Divisional playoff game by a score of 30-22.

DOWN

1. Quarterback from Wake Forest (2019-2020) who made his first NFL appearance as a starter in Week 17 of 2020 when the player referred to in 14 DOWN was hurt. He led the team to a win that day but was knocked out early in the playoff game that followed the next week. He has worn #9 & #13.

2. Undrafted punter from Oregon State (2012-2020) who has made 4 Pro Bowls to date and is a member of the NFL 2010s All-Decade

team. So far he has completed 13 passes for first downs on fake punts. He wears #6.

3. Running back from Georgia (2015-2019) who was a 1st round pick by the Rams. With Los Angeles he was a 3-time Pro Bowler who led the NFL in rushing touchdowns twice. His 58 career rushing scores are tied with Faulk for the most in franchise history. He spent 2020 with Atlanta. He wore #30.

6. The team's first win after coming back to Los Angeles in 2016 was a 9-3 victory over _____.

9. First name of the player referred to in 19 ACROSS.

10. Quarterback from Houston who started the first 9 games the Rams played in their first season back in Los Angeles (2016). After going 4-5 he was benched in favor of the player referred to in 14 DOWN. In 2017 he led the Vikings in a surprising run to the NFC Championship Game. He wore #17.

11. The Super Bowl that the 2018 Rams lost was played in _____.

14. Receiver from USC (2017-2020) who had been a 2nd round pick by the Bills (2013-2016). With the Rams he has had 3 seasons with 85+ catches and 2 with 1,100+ receiving yards. He has worn #17 & #2.

15. Receiver from Rutgers (2014-2016) who had been a 1st round pick by the Titans (2009-2013). With the Rams he had his best season in 2016, with 68 catches and 1,002 receiving yards. He wore #81 & #18.

18. The 2020 Rams were beaten by the _____ in a Divisional playoff game by a score of 32-18.

20. Receiver/special teams player from South Carolina (2016-2018) who was a 4th round pick by the Rams. He was a 2017 Pro Bowler as a returner, leading the NFL with a 27.4 yard average on kickoffs and 399 punt return yards.

He also had 25 catches for the Rams. He wore #10.

24. On their way to the Super Bowl, the 2018 Rams beat the _____ in overtime in the NFC Championship Game by a score of 26-23.

26. The first name of the player referred to in 14 DOWN.

27. Long snapper from Ohio State (2011-2020) who was a 2-time Pro Bowler for the Rams. He never missed a game in his 10 seasons with the team but will play for the Cowboys in 2021. He wore #44.

28. The new home of the Rams is called _____ Stadium.

29. Defensive coordinator who finished his 42-year NFL coaching career with the Rams (2017-2020). He had earlier held the same post with a number of other NFL teams. He had also been the head coach of the Broncos, Bills and Cowboys. His colorful dad was also a fine NFL coach.

30. The first name of the player referred to in 1 DOWN.

32. Defensive lineman from Nebraska (2018) who had been a 1st round pick by the Lions (2010-2014). He played for the Dolphins (2015-2017) before helping the 2018 Rams reach the Super Bowl. He became a Super Bowl Champion with the 2020 Buccaneers. He wore #93.

33. The Rams played in St. Louis for ____ seasons.

34. Undrafted San Diego County and Washington product (2016-2019) who was a 2018 Pro Bowler and started every game for the Rams in both 2018 and 2019. He has gone on to make another 30 starts in his 2 seasons with the Raiders (2019 & 2020). He wore #58.

36. Quarterback from California (2016-2020) who was taken 1st overall by the Rams. He led the 2018 team to the Super Bowl and was a 2-time Pro Bowler for Los Angeles. He did not play quite as well in 2019 or 2020 and was dealt to Detroit for 2021. He wore #16.

39. The Rams did not have a 1st round pick in the 2021draft but their 2nd round pick was this lightning quick but tiny (5'9", 165-pound) receiver from Louisville who had 70 catches for 1,276 yards in 2019.

LOS ANGELES RAMS

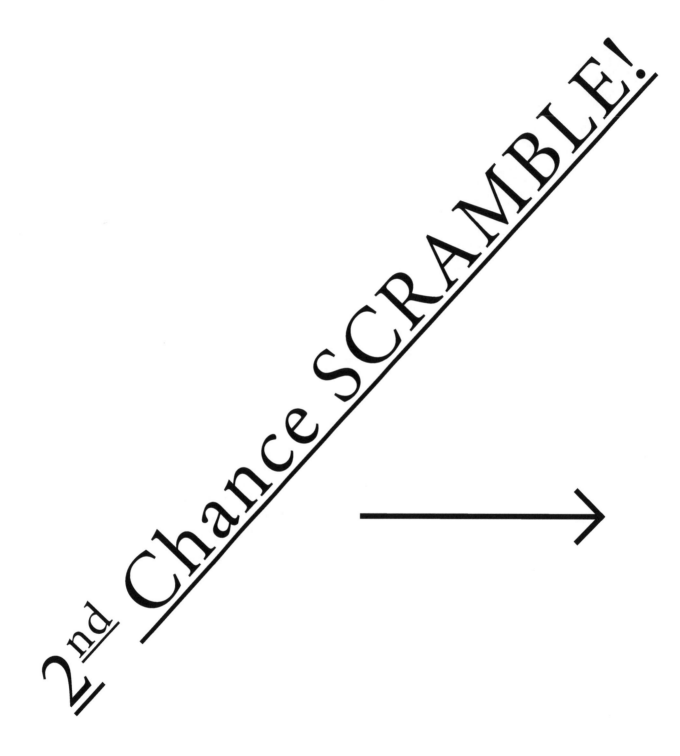

LOS ANGELES RAMS

ACROSS

1. OHHRTIWTW _ _ _ _ _ _ _ _ _
3. EGGR _ _ _ _
4. PUKP _ _ _ _
5. ISREHF _ _ _ _ _ _
7. EROBTR _ _ _ _ _ _
8. EOKRKEN _ _ _ _ _ _ _
12. MVYAC _ _ _ _ _
13. LEEVLCADN _ _ _ _ _ _ _ _ _
16. EERUZNLI _ _ _ _ _ _ _ _
17. ECPOOR _ _ _ _ _ _
19. SCLNFAO _ _ _ _ _ _ _
21. IASRTOPT _ _ _ _ _ _ _ _
22. DNLDOA _ _ _ _ _ _
23. AERSK _ _ _ _ _
25. AESN _ _ _ _
29. STEPRE _ _ _ _ _ _
31. CKOSO _ _ _ _ _
35. EIGHEB _ _ _ _ _ _
37. LIGOWEODN _ _ _ _ _ _ _ _ _
38. FDATFOSR _ _ _ _ _ _ _ _
40. ASEFLS _ _ _ _ _ _
41. XSI _ _ _
42. LSIMCEOU _ _ _ _ _ _ _ _
43. YNENK _ _ _ _ _
44. AALDSL _ _ _ _ _ _

DOWN

1. FOOFRWD _ _ _ _ _ _ _
2. HEERKK _ _ _ _ _ _
3. RYLGUE _ _ _ _ _ _
6. ETLTAES _ _ _ _ _ _ _
9. MWHTAET _ _ _ _ _ _ _
10. KNEEMU _ _ _ _ _ _
11. NATLTAA _ _ _ _ _ _ _
14. OWODS _ _ _ _ _
15. RITTB _ _ _ _ _
18. KEPARCS _ _ _ _ _ _ _
20. RCOPEO _ _ _ _ _ _
24. NSATSI _ _ _ _ _ _
26. JDREA _ _ _ _ _
27. IDQUEACM _ _ _ _ _ _ _ _
28. SFOI _ _ _ _
29. LPSIILPH _ _ _ _ _ _ _ _
30. HNJO _ _ _ _
32. HUS _ _ _
33. EWNTTYNEO _ _ _ _ _ _ _ _ _
34. ETLITOTNL _ _ _ _ _ _ _ _ _
36. FOGF _ _ _ _ _
39. ETLWLA _ _ _ _ _ _

IX

NEW ORLEANS SAINTS

ACROSS

1. Undrafted receiver from Toledo (2005-2013) who was a 2010 Super Bowl Champion for the Saints and had 1,200 receiving yards in 2012. He was a precise route runner and skilled possession receiver rather than a deep threat. He is 5th all-time for the Saints with 38 scoring catches and 6th with 346 receptions. He wore #16.

7. Hall of Fame, Danish-born, left-footed kicker from Michigan State (1982-1994) who was a 4th round pick and a 6-time Pro Bowler for the Saints. His 302 field goals are the most ever for the Saints and his 565 career field goals are the 2nd most in NFL history. No one appeared in more NFL games (382). He wore #7.

8. Undrafted kicker from Notre Dame (2001-2006 & 2009-2010) who had earlier been a 1994 Pro Bowler with the Chargers (1990-2000). His 168 field goals are 2nd most in Saints history and his 478 career field goals are 5th most in NFL history. He served as a kicking mentor on the 2009 team that won a Super Bowl. He wore #3.

9. Defensive tackle from San Diego State (1997-2001) who had been a 5th round pick by the Raiders. With the Saints he was a 2-time Pro Bowler, the NFL sacks leader in 2000 and the NFL Defensive Player of the Year (2000). He is a member of the Saints Hall of Fame. He went on to play 7 more years for Dallas and the Rams. He wore #97.

10. Running back from Tennessee (2017-2019) who was a 3rd round pick by the Saints and has made the Pro Bowl in each of his first 3 seasons. In 2017 he was the NFL Offensive Rookie of the Year. Extremely versatile, he has 2,400 career rushing yards to date and he has caught EXACTLY 81 passes in each season. He wears #41.

11. Tight end from Miami (2010-2014) who was a 3rd round pick and a 4-time Pro Bowler for the Saints. He had 2 years with 1,000+ receiving yards for the Saints and he led the NFL with 16 scoring catches in 2013. His 51 touchdown catches are 2nd most in team history. He has since gone on to play for Seattle and Green Bay. He wore #80.

14. Tight end from USC (1981-1993) who was a 3rd round pick and played only for the Saints. He was a 1987 Pro Bowler and is a member of the Saints Hall of Fame. He made 157 starts for the Saints, including every game in 6 different seasons. His 3,849 career receiving yards put him at #8 on the all-time Saints list. He wore #85.

16. Undrafted kicker from Georgia State (2016-2019) who was a 2019 Pro Bowler for the Saints. His 119 career field goals are the 4th most in team history and he is #1 on the team's all-time accuracy list (87.5%) among those with 100+ tries. He wears #3.

17. The first name of the player referred to in 15 ACROSS.

19. Quarterback from Purdue (1994-1996) who had been a 1st round pick by the Rams (1986-1993) and taken 3rd overall. He led the NFL in touchdown passes twice with the Rams. His best years were behind him with the Saints though, and he went just 17-30 as a starter. He is recalled for a live, televised dust-up with Jim Rome. He wore #17.

20. Kicker from Georgia (2011) who had been a 4th round pick by Seattle (1991-1994) and a Pro Bowler with Carolina (1995-2010), for whom he is #1 all-time with 351 career field goals. He kicked 28 field goals for the Saints in the last of his 21 NFL seasons. His 461 career field goals are 7th most in NFL history. He wore #2.

21. In 2010 the Saints defeated the _____ to become Super Bowl Champions.

23. Receiver from Ohio State (2016-2019) who was a 2nd round pick by the Saints and has made the Pro Bowl in each of his first 3 seasons. He led the NFL in catches in both 2018 and 2019 and he led in receiving yards in 2019. He was also the NFL Offensive player of the year in 2019. He wears #13.

27. The first name of the player referred to in 18 DOWN.

29. The first name of the player referred to in 8 ACROSS.

30. Defensive back from Ohio State (2017-2019) who was a 1st round pick by the Saints and has made 2 Pro Bowls to date (2017 & 2019). He has started 43 out of a possible 48 regular season games and has posted 8 interceptions. He wears #23.

31. Defensive back from Indiana (2008-2011) who was a 2nd round pick by the Saints. He was a 2010 Super Bowl Champion and made an unforgettable, clinching play with a 74-yard touchdown return of an interception late in the game. He has since gone on to play for the Broncos, Raiders, Redskins and Bears. He wore #22.

34. Receiver from Itawamba CC (2000-2006) who had been a 5th round pick by the Chiefs (1996-1999). He was a 4-time Pro Bowler with 4 years of 1,200+ receiving yards for the Saints and he is a member of the team's Hall of Fame. He will be sentenced, however, in April 2020 for his role in a health care fraud case. He wore #87.

36. The Saints finally won their first playoff game by beating the _____ in 2000.

37. The first name of the player referred to in 13 DOWN.

39. Kicker from Cal (1995-2000) who has been a 3rd round pick by the 49ers (1994-1995), for whom he became a Super Bowl Champion when SF trashed the Chargers. His 123 field goals are the 3rd most in Saints history. He made 83% of his field goal tries for the Saints and then went on to kick for 5 other teams. He wore #10.

40. Center from Ohio State (2002-2005) who was a 2nd round pick and a 2-time Pro Bowler for the Saints (2003 & 2005). Unhappy with Saints management, he forced a trade to his hometown Cleveland Browns and played 2 more seasons. He wore #57.

43. Drew Brees went to high school in _____ Texas.

44. Saints head coach (1986-1996) whose teams went 93-78 in the regular season but were 0-4 in the post-season. He is 2nd all-time for the Saints in victories. He later went 32-34 as the head coach of the Colts (1998-2001) and achieved some renown when he went off on his "Playoffs?!... Playoffs?!" rant.

45. Receiver from Tennessee (2002-2005) who was a 1st round pick by the Saints. He had 70 catches for 945 yards in 2005 then went on to play without distinction for 5 other teams (2006-2012). He missed the 2009 season after pleading guilty to a DUI manslaughter charge in Miami. He wore #83.

47. Defensive end from Cal (2011-2019) who was a 1st round pick and has only played for the Saints to date. He has made 5 Pro Bowls and his 87 career sacks are the 2nd most in franchise history. His dad was a 6-time Pro Bowl tight end for the Vikings. He wears #94.

48. Saints head coach (2006-2011 & 2013-2019) whose team has gone 131-77 in the regular season. His 139 total wins are #1 in Saints history.

50. The first name of the player referred to in 1 ACROSS is.

52. The Super Bowl that was won by the Saints was played in the city of _____.

53. Defensive back from Notre Dame (1980-1989) who was a 2nd round pick and a 1987 Pro Bowler for the Saints. He is a member of the Saints Hall of Fame and his 37 interceptions are a franchise record. He went on to play 3 years for the 49ers and Raiders. He died at age 34 of a cocaine-induced heart attack in 1993. He wore #43.

56. The first name of the coach referred to in 26 ACROSS.

58. Center from Oregon (2015-2018) who had earlier been a 2nd round pick by Seattle (2009-2014), for whom he was a 2-time Pro Bowler and a 2014 Super Bowl Champion. With the Saints he was a 2018 Pro Bowler and started 63 out of a possible 64 regular season games. He wore #60.

59. Heisman-winning running back from San Diego and USC (2006-2010) who was a 1st round pick by the Saints and taken 2nd overall. He was a 2008 Pro Bowler and 2010 Super Bowl Champion for New Orleans. He went on to have 1,000-yard rushing seasons with Miami (2011) and Detroit (2013). He wore #25.

60. Linebacker from Arkansas State (2018-2021) who had been a 3rd round pick by the Jets (2012-2015 and 2017). He is known for his amazing durability, having never missed a game in his 10 NFL seasons until week 15 of the 2021 season, when he was added to the Covid list. He had made 62 straight starts for the Saints. He wears #56.

64. Receiver from Oregon State (2014-2016) who was a 1st round pick by the Saints and had 2 seasons with 1,100+ receiving yards. With the Patriots, he had 1,000 receiving yards in 2017 and helped the team reach the Super Bowl. With the Rams in 2018 he had 1,200 receiving yards. He was slowed by injuries in 2019. He wore #10.

65. Undrafted kicker from Oklahoma (2008-2013) who was a 2010 Super Bowl Champion with the Saints. His 82 career field goals are the 5th most in team history. A streak of inconsistency led to his release late in 2013. He went 3 for 3 with the Browns late in 2014 but never connected with another team thereafter. He wore #5.

66. The first name used by the player referred to in 1 DOWN.

67. The Saints were owned from 1985 to 2018 by the much-loved Tom _____.

68. The NFL refers to the Super Bowl that the Saints won by using the Roman numerals _____.

69. Guard from Bloomsburg State (2006-2016) who was a 4th round pick, a 6-time Pro Bowler and a 2010 Super Bowl Champion for the Saints. He started every game in his first 7 seasons with the Saints and started 169 out of a possible 176 regular season games in his 11 seasons in New Orleans. He wore #73.

DOWN

1. Running back from Mississippi (2001-2009) who was a 1st round pick and only played for the Saints. He was a 2-time Pro Bowler and is a member of the Saints Hall of Fame. He is #1 on the all-time Saints list in rushing yards and #2 in rushing touchdowns. His real first name is Dulymus. He wore #26.

2. Hall of Fame offensive tackle from Louisiana Tech (1993-2001) who was a 1st round pick and a 7-time Pro Bowler for the Saints and then was a 4-time Pro Bowler with the Chiefs. He started every game in 6 of his 9 seasons with the Saints. He is a member of both the NFL All-Decade Teams for the 1990s and 2000s. He wore #77.

3. The first name of the player referred to in 32 ACROSS.

4. The first name of the player referred to in 6 DOWN

5. Undrafted defensive back from USC (1997-2002) who was a 2001 Pro Bowler and is a member of the Saints Hall of Fame. His 28 interceptions are the 3rd most in team history. He went on play 6 more seasons with the Dolphins, Chiefs, Jaguars and Giants. He wore #29.

6. Heisman-winning running back from Alabama (2011-2018) who was a 1st round pick and a 2-time Pro Bowler. He is #2 all-time for the Saints in rushing yards and #1 for his 50 rushing touchdowns. In 2019 he made another Pro Bowl for the Ravens with his 3rd career season with 1,000 yards. He wore #22.

9. A live Saint Bernard named _____ was a team mascot that roamed the sidelines for years at Saints home games. He has since been replaced by a human in a dog suit.

12. 5'11", 280 pound running from Pittsburgh (1988-1992) who was a 1st round pick by the Saints. His fierce running style earned him the name "Iron Head." He had his only 1,000-yard rushing season for Atlanta in 1995. He died of a brain tumor at age 39 in 2006. He wore #34.

13. Quarterback from Northwestern State (1985-1992) who came to the Saints after 3 years in the USFL. He led the Saints to their first playoff berth in the 1987 season. He went 49-26 as a starter for the Saints and stands at #4 in team history in completions, passing yards and scoring passes. He wore #3.

15. Receiver from Iowa (1991-1995) who was a 3rd round pick by the Chargers (1998-2000). He had 1,000 receiving yards for the Saints in 1995 and is #9 all-time for the Saints in receiving yards, as well as #10 in scoring catches. He also played well for the Bills (1996-1998). He wore #89.

16. The defending Super Bowl Champion Saints were beaten in a playoff game in Seattle in 2011, highlighted by an incredible 67-yard touchdown during which _____ outmaneuvered and abused 9 Saints defenders.

18. Receiver from Hofstra (2006-2015) who was a 7th round pick, only played for the Saints and was a 2010 Super Bowl Champion. Despite recording 6 seasons with 1,000+ receiving yards, he never made a Pro Bowl. He is #1 in team history in catches, receiving yards and scoring catches. He wore #12.

22. Before the Super Dome was constructed, the Saints played their home games in _____ Stadium.

24. Running back from LSU (1986-1993) who was a 2nd round pick and only played for the Saints. He was a 1989 Pro Bowler when he led the NFL with 1,262 rushing yards. He is #4 all-time for the Saints in rushing yards and he also caught 249 passes. He is a member of the Saints and Louisiana Sports Halls of Fame. He wore #21.

25. Undrafted 5'9" linebacker from Montclair State (1986-1994) who was a 4-time Pro Bowler for the Saints and then made another Pro Bowl with the 1996 Panthers. He is also a member of the Saints Hall of Fame. Head Coach Jim Haslett (1986-1996) referred to him as "the best player I ever coached." He wore #51.

26. Line backer from Georgia Tech (1986-1992) who was a 3rd round pick by the Saints and a 4-time Pro Bowler. He led the NFL in sacks and was the NFL Defensive Player of the Year in 1991. He is yet another member of the Saints Hall of Fame. His 765 career sacks are the 4th most in Saints history. He wore #56.

28. Quarterback from Virginia (2000-2005) who came to the Saints after not playing a down-for the 1999 Packers. He went just 38-44 as a starter for the Saints but is #2 all-time for the Saints in touchdown passes and #3 in both completions and passing yards. He wore #2.

29. Heisman-winning running back and San Diego high school product from Texas (1999-2001) who was a 1st round pick by the Saints and taken 5th overall. He had 2 years with 1,000+ rushing yards for the Saints but had most of his success with the Dolphins, for whom he led the NFL with 1,800 rushing yards in 2002. He wore #34.

32. Offensive tackle from San Diego State (1998-2002) who was a 1st round pick by the Saints and taken 7th overall. He made 1st Team All-Pro in 2000 and did the same with the Rams in 2003. He started 79 out of a possible 80 regular season games for the Saints. He is known for touring across America with his country band. He wore #68.

33. The first name of the player referred to in 23 DOWN.

35. Guard from Nebraska (2008-2011) who was a 5th round pick by the Saints as well as a 2-time Pro Bowler and a 2010 Super Bowl Champion. He started 61 out of a possible 64 regular season games for the Saints before going on to finish up with the Buccaneers (2012-2013). He wore #77.

38. The Saints have their headquarters and training facility in the New Orleans community of _____.

41. Receiver from LSU (1985-1993) who was a 7th round pick and a 1988 Pro Bowler for the Saints. He had 3 years with 1,000+ receiving yards and is a member of the Saints Hall of Fame. He is 2nd all-time in club history in both receptions and receiving yards and 4th in catches. He wore #84.

43. Offensive tackle from Arkansas-Pine Bluff (2013-2019) who was a 3rd round pick and has only played for the Saints. He has made 2 Pro Bowls to date (2018 & 2019). He wears #72.

44. Receiver from Tennessee (2007-2011& 2013-2014).who was a 1st round pick and a 2010

Super Bowl Champion with the Saints. His 25 scoring catches are 10th all-time for the Saints. He signed a big free agent deal with the Chargers for 2012 but was such a bust that he was cut loose after just one year. He wore #17.

45. The first name of the player referred to in 4 ACROSS.

46. Undrafted running back from Illinois (2007-2014) who was a 2010 Super Bowl Champion for the Saints. He led the team in rushing in 2008, 2009 and 2013. In 2013 he led all NFL backs in receiving yards. He is 5th all-time for the Saints in career rushing yards and 4th in rushing touchdowns. He wore #23.

47. The first name of the player referred to in 12 ACROSS.

48. The first name of the player referred to in 28 DOWN.

49. Linebacker from Miami (2008-2013) who came to the Saints after having been a 1st round pick by the Jets (2004-2007), for whom he was the NFL Defensive Rookie of the Year. For the Saint's he was a 2-time Pro Bowler and a 2010 Super Bowl Champion. He missed 5 games in 2012 when details of "Bounty Gate" surfaced. He wore #51.

51. Defensive back from Florida A&M (1987-1993) who was a 7th round pick by the Saints. His 21 career interceptions are 4th most all-time for the Saints. He led the NFL with 198 interception return yards in 1991. He finished up with 3 years in Miami (1994-1996). He wore #28.

52. The first name of the player referred to in 16 DOWN.

53. Quarterback from Miami (1990-1993) who had been a 1st round pick by the Cowboys (1989-1990). He went 23-1as a Miami starter and led the team to a 1987 National Championship. With the Saints, he was 10-9 as a starter. He

is 5th all-time for the Saints in completions, passing yardage and touchdown passes. He wore #4.

54. The first name of the player referred to in 37 ACROSS.

55. Undrafted receiver/kick returner from Assumption (2019) who was a Pro Bowler as a rookie. He led the NFL in punt return yardage and returned one punt for a touchdown. He also had 644 kickoff return yards and 6 catches as a receiver. He wears #11.

57. Running back from Arizona State (1994-19 97) who was a 2nd round pick by the Saints. His best season was 1995 when he had 900 rushing yards. His 2,500 career rushing yards are 10th most in team history and his 21 rushing touchdowns are also 10th highest. He wore #24.

61. The first name of the player referred to in 2 ACROSS.

62. The first name of the player referred to in 20 DOWN.

63. The first name of the coach referred to in 29 ACROSS.

NEW ORLEANS SAINTS

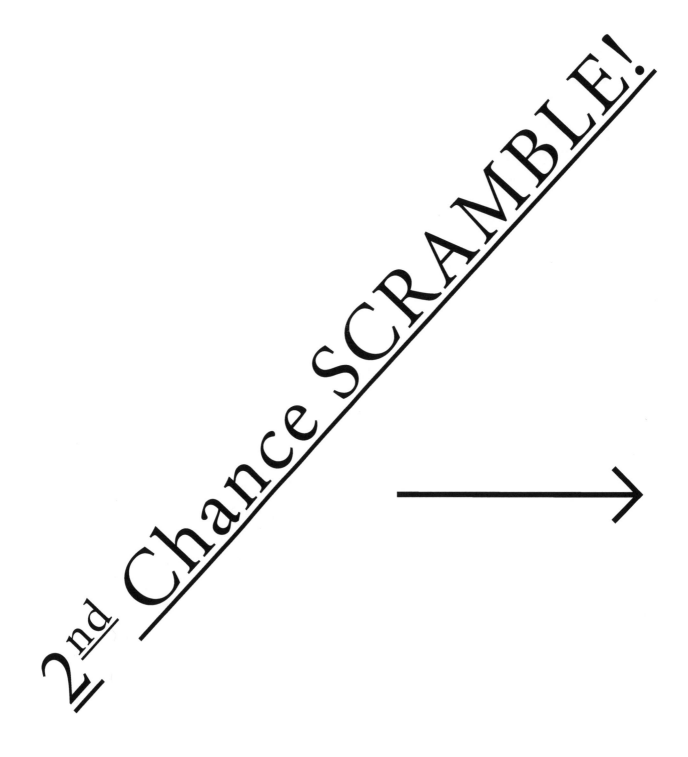

2ⁿᵈ Chance SCRAMBLE!

→

NEW ORLEANS SAINTS

ACROSS		DOWN	
1. OROEM	_ _ _ _ _	1. LCITRASLEM	_ _ _ _ _ _ _ _ _ _
7. NDSNERAE	_ _ _ _ _ _ _ _	2. ROFA	_ _ _ _
8. NREAYC	_ _ _ _ _ _	3. EDVA	_ _ _ _
9. VRLGEO	_ _ _ _ _ _	4. ARMK	_ _ _ _
10. ARKMAA	_ _ _ _ _ _	5. KGNTIH	_ _ _ _ _ _
11. AHRGMA	_ _ _ _ _ _	6. IGMRAN	_ _ _ _ _ _
14. RRBNENE	_ _ _ _ _ _ _	9. UOGBM	_ _ _ _ _
16. UZTL	_ _ _ _	12. EDAWRYH	_ _ _ _ _ _ _
17. RTCYA	_ _ _ _ _	13. HEETRB	_ _ _ _ _ _
19. EETETRV	_ _ _ _ _ _ _	15. AELRY	_ _ _ _ _
20. AASYK	_ _ _ _ _	16. LNHYC	_ _ _ _ _
21. TOLSC	_ _ _ _ _	18. ONCSOLT	_ _ _ _ _ _ _
23. MHSATO	_ _ _ _ _ _	22. NATUEL	_ _ _ _ _ _
27. EKLY	_ _ _ _	24. HLLARIID	_ _ _ _ _ _ _ _
29. LIWL	_ _ _ _	25. ISLLM	_ _ _ _ _
30. OTTELAIMR	_ _ _ _ _ _ _ _ _	26. INGILSWL	_ _ _ _ _ _ _ _
31. ERPORT	_ _ _ _ _ _	28. OKSRBO	_ _ _ _ _ _
34. HRON	_ _ _ _	29. ISIMLWAL	_ _ _ _ _ _ _ _
36. MARS	_ _ _ _	32. LYURET	_ _ _ _ _ _
37. MAS	_ _ _	33. REIC	_ _ _ _
39. RBNIE	_ _ _ _ _	32. SNCIK	_ _ _ _ _
40. EENYTLB	_ _ _ _ _ _ _	32. RAMTIEIE	_ _ _ _ _ _ _ _
43. ATUINS	_ _ _ _ _ _	32. RAMTNI	_ _ _ _ _ _
44. ORAM	_ _ _ _	32. SAAERTDM	_ _ _ _ _ _ _ _
45. RLWLHTSOAT	_ _ _ _ _ _ _ _ _ _	32. CHEAAMM	_ _ _ _ _ _ _
47. NJAORD	_ _ _ _ _ _	32. YOBH	_ _ _ _
48. TPOAYN	_ _ _ _ _ _	32. ATSOHM	_ _ _ _ _ _
50. ALNCE	_ _ _ _ _	32. IMJ	_ _ _
52. MIMIA	_ _ _ _ _	32. EEPRIR	_ _ _ _ _ _
53. MEWYAR	_ _ _ _ _ _	32. LMIVA	_ _ _ _ _
56. MJI	_ _ _	32. IKSNAT	_ _ _ _ _ _
58. GNERU	_ _ _ _ _	32. MUSQAER	_ _ _ _ _ _ _
59. BUSH	_ _ _ _	32. HAWSL	_ _ _ _ _
60. ADVSI	_ _ _ _ _	32. GIRGEE	_ _ _ _ _ _
64. KOCOS	_ _ _ _ _	32. RHISRA	_ _ _ _ _ _
65. LHTAYER	_ _ _ _ _ _ _	32. ESBTA	_ _ _ _ _
66. CUDEE	_ _ _ _ _	32. JNHO	_ _ _ _
67. EOBNNS	_ _ _ _ _ _	32. ALRC	_ _ _ _
68. IXVL	_ _ _ _	32. SNAE	_ _ _ _
69. ANEVS	_ _ _ _ _		

CAROLINA PANTHERS

ACROSS

1. Undrafted quarterback from Louisiana-Lafayette (2003-2009) who came to the NFL with the Saints (1997-2002). He led the Panthers to the 2004 Super Bowl and was a 2005 Pro Bowler. He went 53-37 as a starter for Carolina and is #2 all time for the franchise in passing yards (19,000) and touchdown passes (120). He wore #17.

4. Carolina head coach (2002-2010) and San Diego state product whose teams went 73-71. The 2003 team reached the Super Bowl and as Denver head coach (2011-2014), he made it to the Super Bowl again in 2014. His last head coaching job was a 14-34 disaster with the Bears. His 78 total wins are #2 all-time for Carolina.

7. Undrafted, Scottish-born kicker from Florida State (20l2-2019) who was a 2017 Pro Bowler when he made 29 of 30 field goal tries. He came to Carolina after breaking in with Washington (2009-2011). He has 165 field goals to date for the Panthers, which is the 2nd most in franchise history. He wears #1.

9. Quarterback from Penn State (1995-1998) who was taken 5th overall by Carolina and a 1996 Pro Bowler when he led the team to the NFC Championship Game in just its 2nd season. He went 22-20 as a starter for the Panthers and went on to lead the 2000 Giants to the Super Bowl. He wore #12.

11. Undrafted quarterback from Texas A&M and Houston (20182019) who played in just 2 games as a rookie but started 12 games in 2019 due to injuries to the player referred to in 17 ACROSS. The team went 5-7 in his starts but he played pretty well in view of his inexperience, passing for 3,300 yards. He was dealt to Washington in March 2020. He wore #7.

12. Running back from Memphis (2006-2014) who was a 1st round pick by Carolina, for whom he was a 2009 Pro Bowler when he had his second season with 1,000+ rushing yards. He led the NFL in rushing touchdowns with 18 in 2008. He is #2 on the Panther all-time rushing yards list with 6,800. He wore #34.

15. The first name of the coach referred to in 20 ACROSS.

16. Guard from LSU (2014-2019) who was a 3rd round pick by Carolina and a 5-time Pro Bowler. He made 80 starts for the Panthers in his 6 seasons, including every game for the 2015 team that reached the Super Bowl. He was traded to the Chargers in March 2020. He wore #70.

17. Defensive back from Jacksonville State (1996-2000) who had been a 2nd round pick by the 49ers (1990-1995). He was a 1996 Pro Bowler with Carolina and his 25 career interceptions are #2 all-time for the Panthers. He is the only player with an interception in 5 straight playoff games. He wore #25.

21. Tight end from Mississippi (1996-2002) who had been a 2nd round pick by the 49ers (1989-1993). He played for the Saints (1994-1995) before coming to Carolina, for whom he made 5 Pro Bowls. He is 3rd all-time for the Panthers with 44 touchdown catches and 4th with 3,900 receiving yards. He wore #85.

23. Left-footed kicker from Georgia (1995-2010) who had been a 4th round pick by Seattle (1991-1994). He was a 1996 Pro Bowler when he led the NFL with 37 field goals. He had 32 field goals for the 2015 team that reached the Super Bowl and his 351career field goals are the most in team history. He wore #4.

24. Offensive tackle from USC (2017-2018) who had been taken 4th overall by Minnesota (2012-2016). He made his only Pro Bowl as a rookie and started every game over the next 3 seasons but he never lived up to his draft status. He started every game for the 2017 Panthers but missed all of 2018 due to injury. He wore #75.

26. Heisman-winning quarterback from Florida State (2001-2006) who was just a 4th round pick by Carolina. He had played 7 years of minor league baseball before college and he came to

the Panthers as a 29-year old rookie! He went just 2-17 as a starter for Carolina with way more interceptions than scoring passes. He wore #16.

27. The first name of the player referred to in 26 DOWN.

29. The Panthers have won their division a total of _____ times.

30. Heisman-winning quarterback from Auburn (2011-2019) who was taken 1st overall by Carolina. He made 3 Pro Bowls for the Panthers and led the 2015 team to the Super Bowl when he was the NFL MVP. He made just 2 starts due to injury in 2019 and then signed a one-year deal with the Patriots in July 2020. He wore #1.

34. The Panthers have a 10-4 all-time record against the _____, which is their highest winning percentage against any opponent.

36. The Panthers have just a 1-6 all-time record against the _____, which is their lowest winning percentage against any opponent.

37. Carolina head coach (1999-2001) whose teams went just 8-8, 7-9 and 1-15. He had earlier been the head coach of the 49ers (1989-1996), whom he led to a pair of Super Bowl Championships. In fact, his 108 career victories for San Francisco are the most in the history of that franchise.

39. Defensive end from North Carolina (2002-2009 & 2017-2018) who was taken 2nd overall by Carolina and was a 5-time Pro Bowler. He was the NFL Defensive Rookie of the Year and he helped the team reach the 2004 Super Bowl. 97 of his 159 career sacks came with the Panthers, which are the most in franchise history. He wore #92.

41. Undrafted defensive end from Troy (2012-209) who had first played for 3 other teams. His career took off with Carolina, for whom he had 9+ sacks in each of the past 4 seasons. His 55 career sacks are #4 all-time for the team. He made 14 starts for the 2015 Super Bowl team and is signed for 2020 with the Hills. He wore #97.

43. The first name of the player referred to in 11 ACROSS.

46. Undrafted running back from Lane College (Tennessee) (1997-1999) who had 2,001 rushing yards for Carolina in his 3 seasons. He was traded to the Colts after the 1999 season but was shot to death by his wife in July 2000. He wore #32.

47. Receiver from Michigan State (1996-2004 & 2008-2009) who was a 2nd round pick and a 2-time Pro Bowler for Carolina. He had 3 years with 1,100+ receiving yards for the Panthers. He is #2 all-time for the team in both receiving yards (9,200) and scoring catches (50). He wore #87.

48. Defensive tackle from Purdue (2013-2019) who was a 2nd round pick by Carolina and has made 2 Pro Bowls to date. He has only played for the Panthers and has made 73 career starts, including every game in 3 straight seasons (2015-2017). He had 6 of his 33 career sacks for the 2015 Super Bowl team. He wears #99.

50. Defensive end from Georgia (2007-2017) who was a 3rd round pick and only played for Carolina. He helped the 2015 team reach the Super Bowl and had 6 seasons with 10+ sacks. He made 114 career starts for the Panthers and his 67.5 career sacks are #2 in franchise history. He wore #95.

54. The first name of the player referred to in 7 DOWN.

55. Offensive tackle from Utah (2003-2013) who was taken 8th overall by Carolina and was a 3-time Pro Bowler. He only played for the Panthers and made 167 starts, including every game in 8 of his 11 seasons. He helped the team reach the 2004 Super Bowl with one of his 16-start seasons. He wore #69.

56. The first name of the coach referred to in 34 DOWN.

57. Linebacker from Georgia (2005-2018) who was a 1st round pick by the Panthers and a 3-time Pro Bowler. He made 158 starts for Carolina, including every game for the 2015 Super Bowl team. He is #1 all-time for the Panthers with 789 solo tackles. He started every game for the 2019 Chargers. He wore #47 & #58.

CAROLINA PANTHERS

57. Running back from Auburn (2003-2005) who had been a 4th round pick by Washington (1996-2002), for whom he was a 2-time Pro Bowler and the 1999 NFL leader with 17 rushing touchdowns. He had a career-best 1,444 rushing yards for the 2003 team that made it to the Super Bowl. He wore #48.

58. Hall of Fame linebacker/defensive end from Auburn (1996 & 1998-1999) who had been a 5th round pick by the Rams (1985-1992). He went on to make 2 Pro Bowls with the Steelers (1993-1995) and then was the NFL Defensive Player of the Year with Carolina in 1996 when he led the league with 14.5 sacks. He wore #91.

60. Linebacker from Miami (2007-2013) who was a 1st round pick and a- 3-time Pro Bowler for Carolina. He made just 5 total starts in 2011-2012 due to an Achilles injury and was never the same again, though he did labor through 2 more seasons with the Giants (2014-2015). He wore #52.

61. Receiver from Maryland (2018-2019) who was a 1st round pick by Carolina. After a solid rookie year, he broke out in 2019 with 87 catches for 1,175 yards. His first name is Denniston but he goes by 2 initials. He wears #12.

66. The 1996 Panthers won the first playoff game in the short history of the franchise by beating the _____, 26-17 in the Divisional Round.

68. 360-pound defensive tackle from Maryland (2001-2007) who was a 2nd round pick by Carolina and a 3-time Pro Bowler. He started 79 games for the Panthers, including game for the 2003 Super Bowl team. He was a terrific run-stopper who also had 20 sacks. He made the Pro Bowl again with the 2008 Jets. He wore #77.

69. Defensive back from Ohio State (2004-2012) who was a 1st round pick by Carolina and is the all-time franchise leader in both interceptions (27) and passes defended (98). He played only for the Panthers and made 117 starts. He scored 3 defensive touchdowns and is #5 for Carolina with 440 solo tackles. He wore #20.

DOWN

2. The 2003 Panthers completed their run to the Super Bowl with a 14-3 win over the _____ in the NFC Championship Game.

3. Do-everything running back from Stanford (2017-2019) who was taken 8th overall by Carolina. He had 1,000 rushing yards in 2018 and followed that with an amazing Pro Bowl season in 2019 that featured 1,387 rushing yards and 1,005 receiving yards on 116 catches. Let's not wear this guy out! He wears #22.

4. Receiver from Michigan (2015-2018) who was a 2nd round pick by Carolina. He had 31 catches for the 2015 team that made it to the Super Bowl. His best year was 2017 when he had 63 catches for 840 yards. He spent 2019 with the Colts but played little due to injury. He signed with the Packers in April 2020. He wore #17.

5. The first name of the player referred to in 23 ACROSS.

6. Quarterback from Notre Dame (2010-2013) who was a 2nd round pick by Carolina. He came out early, expecting to go in the 1st round but his cocky manner was off-putting to NFL scouts and executives. Sure enough, he went 1-9 as a starter for the Panthers and later went 0-4 with the Bears. He wore #2.

8. The first name of the player referred to in 6 DOWN.

10. Running back from Michigan (1996-2001) who was born in Zaire and taken 8th overall by the Panthers. He only played for Carolina but injuries were a continuing problem. He was only able to make 35 starts in his 6 seasons. He never made a Pro Bowl and his best season featured 718 rushing yards in 1999. He wore #21.

13. The first name of the player referred to in 24 ACROSS.

14. 5'10', 240-pound running back from Oregon (2008-2017) who was a 1st round pick by Carolina and a 2015 Pro Bowler when he had 989 rushing yards for the team that made it to the Super Bowl.

He had earlier posted a 1,133 yard season in 2009. His 7,300 career rushing yards are #1 in franchise history. He wore #28.

18. The first name of the player referred to in 8 ACROSS.

19. Receiver from Nicholls State (Louisiana) (1995-1998) who had been a 3rd round pick by Tampa Bay (1987-1992), for whom he had 5,000 receiving yards. He had 66 catches for 1,000 yards for Carolina in 1995 and had 570 catches in his 12 year NFL career. He wore #83.

20. Receiver/return specialist from Arizona (1995-2000 & 2002-2003) who had been a 6th round pick by Seattle. He was a 5-time Pro Bowler for Carolina, for whom he returned 5 kickoffs for touchdowns. He is a member of the NFL 1990s All Decade team and is the franchise all-time leader in return yardage. He wore #81.

22. The first name of the player referred to in 13 DOWN.

25. Quarterback from Notre Dame (1996-2000) who had been a 4th round pick by Oakland (1987-1990). He also played for Dallas, Arizona and Jacksonville before coming to Carolina. He made his only Pro Bowl with the Panthers (1999) and went 23-28 as a starter. He is #3 all-time for the team in passing yards. He wore #7.

28. Running back from UCLA (2002-2007) who was a 2nd round pick by Carolina. He had 400 rushing yards for the 2003 team that reached the Super Bowl and then 850 rushing yards in 3 straight seasons (2005-2007). His 3,300 career rushing yards are #4 all-time for the Panthers. He wore #20 & #26.

31. The first name of the player referred to in 2 ACROSS.

32. The first Carolina head coach (1995-1998) whose teams went 30-34, with the 1996 team making it to the NFC Championship Game in just the 2nd year of the existence of the franchise. He later went on to be the first coach of the Houston Texans (2002-2005).

33. The first name of the player referred to in 27 DOWN.

35. Linebacker from Boston College (2012-2019) who was taken 9th overall by Carolina and made 7 Pro Bowls. He only played for the Panthers and was the 2013 NFL Defensive Player of the Year. He led the NFL in tackles twice and is a member of the NFL 2010s All-Decade Team. He made 118 career starts and wore #59.

38. Defensive end from Nebraska (1999 2007) who was a 2nd round pick by Carolina and a 2003 Pro Bowler. He only played for the Panthers and made 106 career starts, including 14 games for the team that made it to the 2004 Super Bowl. He wore #93.

40. The first name of the player referred to in 6 ACROSS.

42. The first name of the coach referred to in 17 DOWN.

44. The Panthers have beaten the _____ 25 times to date which is the most wins they have ever achieved over any opponent.

45 6'5", 245-pound receiver from Florida State (2014-2017) who was a 1st round pick by Carolina. He had 73 catches for 1,008 yards as a rookie but missed all of 2015 due to a torn ACL suffered in the pre-season. He bounced back with 63 catches for 941yards in 2016 and was dealt to Buffalo in 2017. He wore #13.

47. Defensive back from Nebraska (1997-2006) who was a 2nd round pick and only played for Carolina. He made 141 starts, including every game for the 2003 Super Bowl team. His 17 interceptions are #4 all-time for the Panthers and his 608 solo tackles are #4. He also scored 4 defensive touchdowns and wore #30.

49. The first name of the player referred to in 29 ACROSS.

51. Undrafted, 5'9", 245-pound running back from Coastal Carolina (2012-2016) who had earlier played for the Chargers (2008-2011). He was a 3-time Pro Bowler for the Panthers and helped the 2015 team reach the Super Bowl. He was a terrific short-yardage back and a fierce lead blocker. He wore #35.

52. Heisman runner-up receiver from Notre Dame (1996-1998) who played for 2 years in the CFL (1991-1992) and then 3 years with Raiders (1993-1995) before coming to Carolina. With the Panthers he had 1,000 receiving yards in 1998 and then another 1000-yard season with Dallas in 1999. He wore #81.

53. The Panthers were beaten in the 2016 Super Bowl by the _____ by a score of 24-10.

59. Carolina head coach (2011-2019) whose teams went 76-63-1. The 2015 team reached the Super Bowl and his 79 total wins are the most in franchise history. He was named the Washington head coach in January 2020.

62. Tight end from Miami (2011-2019) who had earlier been a 1st round pick by the Bears (2007-2010). With Carolina he was a 3-time Pro Bowler (2014-2016) when he had 3 straight years with 1,000 receiving yards, with 77 catches for the 2015 Super Bowl team. He signed with Seattle in February 2020 and wore #88.

63. The first name of the coach referred to in 3 ACROSS.

64. The first name of the player referred to in 30 ACROSS.

65. The first name of the player referred to in 1 ACROSS.

CAROLINA PANTHERS

2nd Chance SCRAMBLE!

$\longrightarrow$

XXVI

CAROLINA PANTHERS

ACROSS

1. HEMLEDOM _ _ _ _ _ _ _ _
4. OFX _ _ _
7. OGAN _ _ _ _
9. LCOSLNI _ _ _ _ _ _ _
11. NLELA _ _ _ _ _
12. IAILMLSW _ _ _ _ _ _ _ _
15. EORGEG _ _ _ _ _ _
16. RNUTER _ _ _ _ _ _
17. ASVID _ _ _ _ _
21. SLAWL _ _ _ _ _
23. SAAYK _ _ _ _ _
24. LIKLA _ _ _ _ _
26. NKWEEI _ _ _ _ _ _
27. EKMI _ _ _ _
29. IXS _ _ _
30. ONEWTN _ _ _ _ _ _
34. ALCSNRAID _ _ _ _ _ _ _ _ _
36. ELERSEST _ _ _ _ _ _ _ _
37. ISEFTRE _ _ _ _ _ _ _
39. PESEPPR _ _ _ _ _ _ _
41. NAISODD _ _ _ _ _ _ _
43. RHCIS _ _ _ _ _
46. ALEN _ _ _ _
47. DMHAMUAM _ _ _ _ _ _ _ _
48. THSOR _ _ _ _ _
50. NONSJHO _ _ _ _ _ _ _
54. JIYMM _ _ _ _ _
55. GROSS _ _ _ _ _
56. NOR _ _ _
57. SIDAV _ _ _ _ _
57. VAIDS _ _ _ _ _
58. NGEREE _ _ _ _ _ _
60. ESNBAO _ _ _ _ _ _
61. ORMOE _ _ _ _ _
66. OOBWYSC _ _ _ _ _ _ _
68. KIJENNS _ _ _ _ _ _ _
69. GMLEAB _ _ _ _ _ _

DOWN

2. SGAELE _ _ _ _ _ _
3. EACRMYCFF _ _ _ _ _ _ _ _ _
4. NHSCSUEF _ _ _ _ _ _ _ _
5. IRMAO _ _ _ _ _
6. SENCAUL _ _ _ _ _ _ _
8. MTI _ _ _
10. BIABAAUKTKA _ _ _ _ _ _ _ _ _ _ _
13. RFED _ _ _ _
14. REATWTS _ _ _ _ _ _ _
18. LEKY _ _ _ _
19. RREICRA _ _ _ _ _ _ _
20. TSBAE _ _ _ _ _
22. VTSEE _ _ _ _ _
25. RLEEUINBE _ _ _ _ _ _ _ _ _
28. EFSTOR _ _ _ _ _ _
31. YREKR _ _ _ _ _
32. ERAPSC _ _ _ _ _ _
33. KEMI _ _ _ _
35. ELCUKYH _ _ _ _ _ _ _
38. UREKCR _ _ _ _ _ _
40. EICR _ _ _ _
42. MOD _ _ _
44. NTASSI _ _ _ _ _ _
45. IMEJNBAN _ _ _ _ _ _ _ _
47. EMIRTN _ _ _ _ _ _
49. OHTASM _ _ _ _ _ _
51. TTOELRB _ _ _ _ _ _ _
52. LISIMA _ _ _ _ _ _
53. ROOCSNB _ _ _ _ _ _ _
59. AREIRV _ _ _ _ _ _
62. LONES _ _ _ _ _
63. HONJ _ _ _ _
64. SRKI _ _ _ _
65. EAKJ _ _ _ _

ARIZONA CARDINALS

ACROSS

1. Receiver from Notre Dame (2012-2016) who was a 1st round pick by Arizona. He had 1,000 receiving yards in 2012 and 242 career catches for the Cardinals but didn't really live up to his lofty draft status. He managed just 24 more catches with the Vikings, Patriots and Redskins (2016-2018). He wore #15.

4. Defensive end / linebacker from Syracuse (2016-2019) who had been a 1st round pick by the Patriots (2012-2015), for whom he was a 2015 Super Bowl Champion. He has made 2 Pro Bowls for Arizona to date and he led NFL with 17 sacks in 2017. He is a member of the NFL 2010s All-Decade Team. He wears #55.

7. Kicker from Illinois (2003-2009) who had been a 6th round pick by the Bengals (2000-2002). He was a 2005 Pro Bowler for the Cardinals when he was successful on 40 of 42 field goal tries. His 161 field goals are the 2nd most in franchise history. He wore #1.

8. Kicker from Arizona State (2018-2019) who had been a 7th round pick by the Ravens. 2019 was his first full year with Arizona and he responded with 31 field goals in 35 attempts. He has been re-signed for 2020. He wears #5.

9. The first name of the coach referred to in 14 ACROSS.

10. Kicker from Texas (2017-2018) who had previously played for the Browns (1999-2012) and 49ers (2013-2016). He made a career-high 32 field goals for the Cardinals in 2017 at age 42. His 441 career field goals are the 8th most in NFL history. He wore #4.

12. Cardinal head coach (2000-2003) who took over when the coach referred to in 17 ACROSS was fired in mid-season 2000. His teams went just 1-8, 7-9, 5-11 and 3-12. He had earlier been the Arizona defensive coordinator (1996-2000).

16. Undrafted kicker from Clemson (2014-2 016) whose 78 field goals are 6th all-time for the Cardinals. He kicked a 60-yarder for Arizona in 2016 and has since played for the Jets, Jaguars and Buccaneers. He wore #7.

18. Cardinal head coach (2013-2017) whose 50 career wins are the most in team history (against just 32 losses, which is pretty special for this franchise). He chose to take a year off in 2018 but came back in 2019 to lead the Buccaneers to a 7-9 record.

20. Undrafted quarterback and Arena Leaguer from Northern Iowa (2005-2009) who became a star and Super Bowl Champion with the Rams (1998-2003). He came SO close to winning that 2009 Super Bowl with Arizona. He is 5th all-time for the Cardinals in both passing yards (15,843) and touchdown passes (100). He wore #13.

23. The first name of the coach referred to in 12 DOWN.

26. Cardinal head coach (1994-1995) whose teams went 8-8 and 4-12. He first rose to prominence as the ornery defensive coordinator of the Super Bowl Champion 1985 Bears. Friction with Ditka made him eager to become the head coach of the Eagles. His Philadelphia teams went 43-35 but had no playoff wins.

27. Cardinal head coach (1990-1993) whose teams went just 20-44. He was hired based on his success as an offensive line coach and coordinator for the Redskins (1981-1989), whom he helped to win 2 Super Bowls.

29. Running back from Ohio State (2009-2012) who was a 1st round pick and only played for Arizona. He had 2,400 career rushing yards (1,047 in 2011) and his 24 rushing touchdowns are 10th-most all-time for the Cardinals. His real first name is Chris but he goes by a nickname. He wore #26.

30. The first name of the coach referred to in 10 DOWN.

32. Cardinal head coach (1996-2000) whose teams went 29-44, with one winning season (9-7 in 1998). He had earlier earned a reputation as a defensive coordinator for the Bears (1986-1993) and Colts (1994-1995).

34. The first name of the player referred to in 24 Across.

36. Dynamic, Heisman-winning quarterback from Oklahoma (2019) who was taken 1st overall by Arizona. The team went just 5-10-1 in his rookie year but he was fun to watch and he supplied hope for the future. The team's offense is designed to take advantage of his special skills. Let's hope he stays healthy! He wears #1.

37. The first name of the player referred to in 31 DOWN.

40. Defensive back from LSU (2011-2019) who was taken 5th overall by Arizona and has only played for the Cardinals to date. He has made 8 Pro Bowls and is a member of the NFL 2010s All-Decade team. His 25 interceptions are 7th most all-time for the Cardinals. He wears #21.

44. Defensive end from Florida State (2004-2014) who was a 3rd round pick and only played for Arizona. He was a 3-time Pro Bowler and made 156 career starts, including every game for the 2008 Super Bowl team and for 7 other Cardinal squads. He had 40 career sacks and wore #90.

45. The first name of the player referred to in 5 ACROSS.

46. Defensive back from USC (1987-1992) who was a 2nd round pick and 3-time Pro Bowler for Arizona. He went on to make 3 more Pro Bowls with the 49ers and became a Super Bowl Champion in that 1995 demolition of the Chargers. He had 20 with the Cardinals and 20 with the 49ers. He wore #46.

47. Receiver from Auburn (1995-2002) who was a 2nd round pick by Arizona. He had 1,000+ receiving yards in both 1997 and 1998 and 3 years with 75+ catches. His 493 career catches are 5th all-time for the Cardinals and his 6,579 receiving yards are #7. He wore #81.

50. Receiver from Ohio State (1999-2002) who was taken 8th overall by Arizona. He had 1,100 receiving yards in 2000 and he had his only Pro Bowl season in 2001 when he led the NFL with 1,598 receiving yards. He had one more good year

with the 2003 Chargers but his career was hurt by his evident disinterest. He wore #89.

52. Defensive end from Miami (2008-2016) who was a 2nd round pick by Arizona and a 2-time Pro Bowler. He made 120 starts for the Cardinals, including every game for the 2008 Super Bowl team. He went on to make 3 more Pro Bowls for the Jaguars (2017-2019) and he is a member of the NFL 2010s All-Decade Team. He wore #93.

55. The first name of the player referred to in 24 DOWN.

56. Kicker from Michigan (2010-2013) who had already played 8 seasons for 5 other teams before coming to Arizona. He kicked 98 of his 332 NFL field goals with the Cardinals, 4th most in franchise history. He has done sideline and color commentary on both NFL and NCAA telecasts for CBS. He wore #4 & and #13.

58. Punter from Pitt (2017-2019) who had already played for the 49ers (2004-2014}, Browns (2015) and Panthers (2016) before arriving in Arizona. He has made 3 Pro Bowls to date and his 1,290 punts are the 4th most in NFL history. He wears #4.

59. Arizona's most recent post-season win came in a 26-20 overtime conquest of the _____ in 2016.

60. Undrafted kicker from The Citadel (1991-1996) whose 114 field goals are 3rd most all-time for the Cardinals. He had a career-best 30 field goals in 1995 and 224 career field goals in 12 NFL seasons. He wore #5.

61. The first name of the player referred to in 26 ACROSS.

62. The first name of the player referred to in 1 DOWN.

63. The 2008 Super Bowl team beat the _____ (30-24) in the NFC Wild Card Round.

ARIZONA CARDINALS

DOWN

1. Receiver from Pitt (2004-2019) who was taken 3rd overall by Arizona and is a lock for the Hall of Fame. He has made 11 Pro Bowls so far and is the franchise all time leader in catches (1,378), scoring catches (120) and receiving yards (17,083). He has led the NFL twice in both catches and scoring catches. He wears #11.

2. Linebacker from Auburn (2004-2009, 2013 & 2017) who was a 2nd round pick by Arizona. He helped the team reach the 2009 Super Bowl and he made 113 career starts for the Cardinals. In 2010 he ended an overtime play-off game by returning an Aaron Rodgers fumble for a touchdown. He wore #56.

3. Receiver from-Pittsburg State (Kansas) (2014-2017) who was a 3rd round pick by Arizona. In 2015 he had 65 catches for 1,003 yards. After spending 2018 with the Ravens he moved on to the Bills for 2019 and had another 1000-yard season. His namesake was a hero to the abolitionist movement. He wore #12.

4. Running back from Northern Iowa (2015-2019) who was a 3rd round pick by Arizona and a 2016 Pro Bowler when he had a career-best 1,239 rushing yards. He is #4 in Cardinal history in rushing touchdowns (33) and 10th in rushing yards (3,128). He was dealt to Houston in 2020 to get DeAndre Hopkins. He wore #31.

5. The first name of the player referred to in 21 DOWN.

6. Quarterback from Arizona State (1997-2002) who was a 2nd round pick by Arizona. He only had a 30-52 record as a starter for the Cardinals but is #3 all-time for the franchise in passing yards (17,622) and #6 in touchdown passes (90). He went on to make a Pro Bowl with Denver (2005). He wore #16.

7. Quarterback from UCLA (2018) who was a 1st round pick by Arizona. He went 3-10 as a starter for a bad Cardinal team and was dealt to Miami in 2019. He didn't play well for the Dolphins either and questions arose as to his work ethic. It will be hard for him to recover and avoid being tagged as a "bust". He wore #3.

11. Cardinal head coach (2019) whose team went just 5-10-1 but was still entertaining and auspicious. He had been a star quarterback at Texas Tech and was their head coach (2013-2018). He is implementing in Arizona a modified version of the "air raid" offense he mastered in Lubbock.

12. Cardinal head coach (2007-2012) who guided the team to the 2009 Super Bowl. His 49 career wins are the 2nd most in franchise history. As the head coach of the Titans, he went 2-14 in 2014 and then was fired in mid-season 2015 with the team at 1-6. He went on to be the Charger offensive coordinator (2016-2019).

14. Cardinal head coach (2004-2006) whose teams went just 6-101 5-11 and 5-11. He is perhaps best known for a post-game rant regarding a loss to the Bears in which he said "they are who we thought they are!" He had earlier gone 97-62 as the Viking head coach and taken them to 2 NFC Championship Games.

15. Heisman-winning quarterback from USC (2013-2017) who had been taken first overall by the Bengals (2003-2010). He resurrected his career with Arizona by achieving a 38-21-1 record as a starter. He is 4th in franchise history in both passing yards (16,782) and touchdown passes (105). He wore #3.

17. The first name of the player referred to in 34 ACROSS.

19. The first name of the player referred to in 4 ACROSS.

21. On the way to the Super Bowl, the 2008 Cardinals beat the _____ (32-25) in the NFC Championship Game.

22. Running back from Georgia (1993-1995) who was a Heisman finalist and taken 3rd overall by Arizona. He had 1,070 rushing yards in 1995 and went on to have 3 more 1,000-yard seasons with the 49ers (1997-2003). He finished his 10-year NFL career with 7,900 rushing yards. He wore #20.

XXX

24. Defensive back from Southern (1991-2000) who was a 3rd round pick by Arizona and a 7-time Pro Bowler. He is a member of the NFL 1990s All-Decade Team and the Cardinal Ring of Honor. His 46 career interceptions are the 2nd most in franchise history. His first name comes from Roman mythology. He wore #35.

25. Fullback from Stephen F. Austin (1990-1998) who was a 5th round pick by Arizona and a 2-time Pro Bowler. He had 1,700 rushing yards for the Cardinals but his real value was as a receiver. His 535 catches are the 3rd most in team history and his 827 career catches are #1 in NFL history by a running back. He wore #37.

28. Left-handed, Heisman-winning quarterback from USC (2006-2009) who was a 1st round pick by Arizona but just never developed. He went 7-10 as a starter for the Cardinals and had more interceptions than touchdown passes (15/21). After leaving Arizona, he played in just 4 more NFL games. He wore #7.

31. The 2009 Super Bowl between the Cardinals and Steelers was played in the city of _____.

33. Receiver from Michigan (2007-2010) who was a 5th round pick by Arizona. He had his best season for the 2008 Super Bowl team when he had 77 catches for 1,006 yards. He had a total of 187 catches for the Cardinals and then 61 more for the 2011 Chiefs. He wore #15.

35. En route to the Super Bowl, the 2008 Cardinals disposed of the _____ (33-13) in the NFC Divisional Round.

38. Defensive back from Washington (2017-2019) who was a 2nd round pick by Arizona and has already made 2 Pro Bowls. In 2018 he returned a fumble for a touchdown in a 27-17 loss to Minnesota. His real first name is Bishard but he goes by a nickname his mom gave him because he was a chubby baby. He wears #36.

39. Quarterback from Notre Dame (1993-1994) who had been a 4th round pick by the Raiders. He went 9-12 as a starter for Arizona and is 10th all-time for the Cardinals in passing yardage (4,709). He went on to be a 1999 Pro Bowler with Carolina. He wore #7.

41. Defensive back from North Carolina State (2001-2012) who was a 3rd round pick and only played for Arizona. He was a 5-time Pro Bowler and made 162 career starts, including every game in 6 seasons. His 27 interceptions are the 6th most in franchise history and he is a member of the Cardinal Ring of Honor. He wore #22.

42. Receiver from Syracuse who came to Arizona from the Jets (1990-1994). He was a 1997 Pro Bowler for the Cardinals when he had a career-best 97 catches for 1,584 years. The film "Jerry Maguire" contained game footage of this player and Cuba Gooding Jr. wore his #85.

43. Left-footed kicker from South Florida (2001-2003) who was a 4th round pick by Arizona. He kicked just 34 field goals for the Cardinals but is known for tearing an ACL after landing awkwardly in a post-kick celebration. His older brother, Martin, had field goals and was a 2003 Super Bowl Champ with the Bucs. He wore #7.

48. From 1988 through 2005, the Cardinals played their home games in _____

49. Defensive back from Presbyterian (South Carolina) (2012-2019) who was a 6th round pick by Arizona. He was a 3-time Pro Bowler as a special teamer with a special knack for blocking kicks. He played in 96 games for Arizona before finishing with the Falcons, Ravens and Patriots (2018-2019).

50. Since 1962 the Cardinals have been owned by the _____ family.

51. Running back from Miami (2006-2008) who taken 4th overall by the Colts (1999-2005). He is their all-time leader with 9,000 career rushing yards. With Arizona, he had 1,100+ rushing yards in both 2006 and 2007 and then supplied 500 yards for the 2008 Super Bowl team. He wore #32.

53. Receiver from Florida State (2003-2009) who was a 2nd round pick by Arizona and a 3-time Pro Bowler. He had 4 years for the team with 1,000+ receiving yards, including the 2008 Super Bowl squad. He went on to be a Super Bowl Champ with the 2012 Ravens and had 2 more 1,000-yard seasons with the 49ers. He wore #81.

54. The first name of the player referred to in 21 ACROSS.

57. The Cardinals won their first post-season game since 1947 when they dispatched _____ (20-7) in 1999.

ARIZONA CARDINALS

ARIZONA CARDINALS

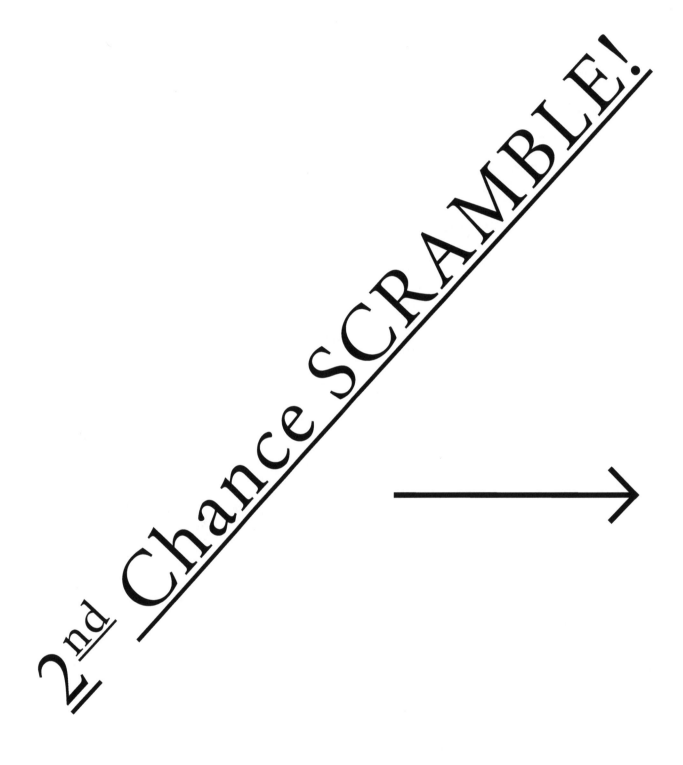

2nd Chance SCRAMBLE!

XXXIV

ARIZONA CARDINALS

1. LYODF _____

4. SJOEN _____

7. KSCARRE _____

8. EOZANLGZ _____

9. OEJ ___

10. ODNWAS _____

13. IGSCMNIN _____

16. ARACOZNAT _____

18. AASNRI _____

20. ERWNRA _____

23. EKN ___

26. NRYA ____

27. LGBUE _____

29. LLSWE _____

30. FLCIF _____

32. NOIBT _____

34. JYA ___

36. RUAMRY _____

37. ROB ___

40. NOTPRSEE _____

44. COKTTDE _____

45. LIHP ____

46. DDNMOACL _____

47. DRNSASE _____

50. OOBNTS _____

52. PAMCELBL _____

55. NIADAR _____

56. YELEF _____

58. LEE ___

59. CKSPEAR _____

60. VAISD _____

61. GGER _____

62. RRALY _____

63. FSOCANL _____

1. IEZFAGDTLR _____

2. YNSDAB _____

3. WBONR _____

4. SJNONOH _____

5. VTSEE _____

6. PRMELMU _____

7. NRSEO _____

11. SKNYUBRGI _____

12. UTWEHISNHN _____

14. NREEG _____

15. PALRME _____

17. MIT ___

19. ELNI ____

21. ELGSAE _____

22. STHEAR _____

24. IWIMLALS _____

25. NECTSER _____

28. NERATLI _____

31. PAMTA _____

33. SRTAEOBN _____

35. PHSERTAN _____

38. KBEAR _____

39. NUEEILRBE _____

41. NIOLSW _____

42. TMAAIARGC _____

43. NBDOIL _____

48. NESLIUDV _____

49. EBTEHL _____

50. LBDWELI _____

51. EMSJA _____

53. OREMO _____

54. EKYRL _____

57. LALDSA _____

DALLAS COWBOYS

ACROSS

1. Tight end from Tennessee (2003-2017 and 2019) who was a 3rd round pick. He was an 11-time Pro Bowler and is the all-time franchise leader in both catches (1,225) and receiving yards (12,977). He "retired" to be a color man on MNF but it was an awkward transition. He came back to play one more year. He wore #82.

6. Running back from Ohio State (2016-2021) who was a 1st round pick and has been a 3-time Pro Bowler and 2-time NFL rushing leader. He has 4 seasons with 1,000+ rushing yards to date and is #3 all-time for Dallas in both rushing yards (7,386) and rushing touchdowns (56). He wears #21.

8. Wide-out from Oklahoma (2020-2021) who was a 1st round pick and has been extremely productive in both of his NFL seasons. He had 74 catches for 935 yards as a rookie and then 79 catches for 1,102 yards in 2021. A brilliant career seems within his grasp. He wears #88.

14. Linebacker from Penn State (2010-2020) who was a 2nd round pick and only played for Dallas. He was a 2-time Pro Bowler and is #8 all-time for the Cowboys with 521 solo tackles, despite missing all of 2014 with a torn ACL. He also had 14 interceptions, with two returned for touchdowns. He wore #50.

15. Guard from Notre Dame (2014-2021) who was a 1st round pick and has made 7 Pro Bowls to date. He started 16 games in 6 of his 8 seasons and has made 120 starts in all. He wears #70.

16. Wide-out from Monmouth (2006-2013) who, though undrafted, was a 2-time Pro Bowler for Dallas and the NFL leader in receiving yards in 2009. He holds the team record for most receiving yards in a game (250 vs. the Chiefs) and he also had 1000+ receiving yards in 2010. He wore #14.

17. The first name of the player referred to in 9 DOWN.

18. Dallas head coach (1998-1999) whose teams went 10-6 and 8-8. He went on to guide the Bills (2010-2012) to 3 last-place finishes in the AFC East. He also served as the offensive coordinator for the Dolphins, Chiefs and Jets.

19. The first name of the player referred to in 6 ACROSS.

20. 6'7", 345-pound offensive tackle from Michigan State (1998-2009) who was a 2nd round pick by Dallas and a 5-time Pro Bowler. He started all 16 games in 10 of his 12 seasons with the Cowboys. He finished up with Pittsburgh in 2010 and again started every game. He wore #76.

26. The first name of the player referred to in 7 DOWN.

27. Undrafted kicker from Missouri Western State (2020-2021) who began with the Rams (2012-2019), for whom he made 201 field goals (82%) and was a 2017 Pro Bowler. He has also made 82% of his field goal tries with Dallas, succeeding on 63 of his 76 attempts, though he has missed 9 PAT kicks. He has worn #4 and #2.

28. Offensive lineman from Texas (2007-2010) who had been a 1st round pick by the Cardinals (2001-2006). He was a 3-time Pro Bowler for Dallas and later moved on to help the 49ers reach the 2012 Super Bowl. He wore #68.

30. The first name of the player referred to in 14 DOWN.

32. Tight end from Wyoming (1990-1995) who had been a 6th round pick by the Cardinals (1985-1989). With Dallas he was a 5-time Pro Bowler and 3-time Super Bowl Champion (1993, 1994 and 1996). He was not a great blocker but did excel at getting downfield. He wore #84.

33. Defensive end from UTEP (1989-1997) who was a 4th round pick and only played for Dallas. He was a 5-time Pro Bowler, a 3-time Super Bowl Champion (1993, 1994 and 1996) and a 1996 Pro Bowler. He recorded 59 career sacks and he led Dallas defensive linemen in tackles for 7 straight seasons. He wore #92.

35. Undrafted punter from East Carolina (1993-1996) who was a 2-time Super Bowl Champion for Dallas (1994 and 1996). He led the NFL in punts

downed inside the 20-yard line in each of his 4 seasons with the Cowboys. He finished up with the Lions (1997-2003). He wore #19.

39. Defensive back from Kansas State (2003-2011) who was a 1st round pick by Dallas and a 2-time Pro Bowler. His 32 interceptions are #7 in franchise history and he led the team in this category 5 times. He went on to Cincinnati (2012-2014) and, finally, Minnesota (2015-2017). He wore #41.

41. Running back from Auburn (1990-1994) who had been a 5th round pick by Seattle. He was a 2-time Super Bowl Champion for Dallas (1993 and 1994). Though he had just 75 carries for the Cowboys, he excelled as a special teamer and as a lead blocker for Emmitt Smith. He had done the same for Bo Jackson at Auburn. He wore #34.

42. Wide-out from USC (2004-2005) who had been drafted #1 overall by the Jets (1996-1999). He had two years with 1,000+ receiving yards for New York and then two more with Tampa Bay (2000-2003), becoming a Super Bowl Champion in 2003. He had 900 receiving yards for Dallas in 2004 and 800 in 2005. He wore #19.

45. Quarterback from Washington State (2005-2006) who had been taken 1st overall by the Patriots (1993-2001), whom he led to the 1997 Super Bowl. He became a Super Bowl Champion in 2002 as a back-up to Tom Brady. After a stop in Buffalo (2002-2004), he came to Dallas and went 12-10 as a starter. He wore #11.

46. Linebacker from Penn State (2021) who was a 1st round pick and had a sensational rookie year. He started every game, made 64 solo tackles and a remarkable 20 tackles for loss. In addition, he had 30 hits on quarterbacks. He wears #11.

50. Dallas head coach (2007-2010) who won two NFC East titles while compiling a 35-24 record with the Cowboys. He had earlier held head coaching jobs with Denver (1993-1994) and Buffalo (1998-2000). He also had successful tenures as a defensive coordinator for 8 NFL teams. His colorful dad was all Texas and also a fine NFL coach.

52. The 2009 Cowboys blew out an _____ team in a Wild Card Game by a score of 34-14.

52. The first name of the player referred to in 10 DOWN.

53. Dallas head coach (2000-2002) who led the team to a woeful cumulative record of 15-33. He had earlier helped the Cowboys win 3 Super Bowls (1993, 1994 and 1996) as a defensive coach. He came back to coach the Dallas defensive backs (2008-2011).

56. Dallas head coach (1994-1997) who led the team to a Super Bowl Championship in 1996 and posted a 40-24 career record. He is a member of the College Football Hall of Fame on the strength of his success at Oklahoma (1973-1985), where he won 3 National Championships.

57. Wide-out from Alabama (2018-2021) who had been a 1st round pick by Oakland (2015-2018), for whom he was a 2-time Pro Bowler with a pair of seasons in which he had 1,000+ receiving yards. Dealt to the Cowboys in mid-2018, he has also made 2 Pro Bowls with Dallas and recorded two more 1,000+ seasons. He wears #19.

59. Heisman runner-up wide out from Notre Dame (1999-2001) who first played in the CFL (1991-1992), with Oakland (1993-1995) and then with Carolina (1996-1998) before finally coming to Dallas. He had 1,000+ receiving yards for the 1998 Panthers and the 1999 Cowboys. He wore #81.

63. Running back from Oklahoma (2011-2014) who was a 3rd round pick by Dallas. In 2014 he was a Pro Bowler, the NFL Offensive Player of the Year and the NFL leader in rushing yards with 1,845. He signed a huge deal with Philadelphia for 2015 but was a disappointment. He was out of the NFL at age 29) He wore #30 and #29.

64. The first name of the player referred to in 35 ACROSS.

65. Dallas head coach (1989-1993) who went 1-15 in his first season but went on to lead the team to Super Bowl Championships in both 1993 and 1994. He had earlier come to prominence as a college coach, winning a National Championship with Miami in 1987. He has long been a fixture as a Fox studio analyst.

68. Hall of Fame quarterback (both College and NFL) from Oklahoma and UCLA (1989-2000) who was taken 1st overall by Dallas. He only played for the Cowboys and was a 6-time Pro Bowler and 3-time Super Bowl Champion (1993, 1994 and 1996). He wore #8. He has teamed with Joe Buck for years as color man on Fox.

70. Defensive tackle from Maryland (1991-1995) who was drafted 1st overall by Dallas. He made his only Pro Bowl in 1993 but his superb play as a run-stopper helped the Cowboys win those 3 Super Bowls (1993, 1994 and 1996). He went on to play for the Raiders (1996-1999) and Packers (2000). He wore #67.

71. Diva, Hall of Fame, wide-out from Tennessee-Chattanooga (2006-2008) who had been a 3rd round pick by the 49ers (1996-2003), for whom he was a 2-time Pro Bowler. After helping the Eagles reach a Super Bowl (2005), he came to Dallas and had 1,000+ receiving yards in each of his 3 seasons. He wore #81.

DOWN

2. Dallas offensive coordinator (1991-1993) who helped the team win two Super Bowls (1993 and 1994). He went on to post a 49-59 mark as the head coach in Washington (1994-2000) and then a 9-23 record in Oakland (2004-2005). With San Diego (2007-2012), his truly talented team also underachieved.

3. Defensive end from North Carolina (1998-2008) who was a 1st round pick by Dallas. He made his only Pro Bowl in 2007, when he was the NFL Comeback Player of the Year. He had 77 sacks for the Cowboys, as well as 21 forced fumbles and scoring returns of 87 and 98 yards. He wore #98.

4. The first name of the player referred to in 28 DOWN.

5. Running back from Notre Dame (2004-2007) who was a 2nd round pick by Dallas and a member of the NFL All-Rookie Team when he rushed for 800 yards. He had 900 yards in 2005 and then had his only 1,000-yard season in 2006. He went on to have two more solid seasons in Seattle (2008 & 2009). He wore #21.

7. Offensive tackle from Central State (1991-2000) who was a 3rd round pick by Dallas, a 4-time Pro Bowler and a 3-time Super Bowl Champion (1993, 1994 and 1996). He made 14+ starts in 8 of his 10 seasons with the Cowboys. He wore #79.

9. Undrafted, courageous 5'8", 175-pound slot receiver from SMU (2012-2018) who had 319 catches for 3,200 yards and 23 touchdowns for Dallas. With Buffalo (2020-2021), he has been even more productive. He has been outspoken in his refusal to be vaccinated. He wore #11.

10. Defensive back from Alabama (2020-2021) who was 2nd round pick and a 2021 Pro Bowler when he led the NFL with 11 interceptions and two scoring returns. His older brother is a Pro Bowl receiver with nearly 600 career catches. He has worn #7 and #27.

11. Undrafted kicker from Oklahoma State (2011-2017) who was a 2015 Pro Bowler for Dallas. His 186 field goals are the most in team history and he succeeded at a rate of 88%. With Minnesota (2018-2020), his accuracy slipped to 80%. He wore #5.

12. Undrafted punter from Cal (2021) who started with Jacksonville (2012-2015) and then moved on to Tampa Bay (2016-2018) and Houston (2019-2020). With Dallas, he finally made his first Pro Bowl in 2021, averaging a career-best 48.4 yards per punt. He wears #5.

13. The 2014 Cowboys defeated the _____ in a Wild Card Game by a score of 24-20.

21. Hall of Fame guard from Sonoma State (1994-2005) who was a 2nd round pick by Dallas, a 1996 Super Bowl Champion and a 10-time Pro Bowler. He is a member of the Cowboy Ring of Honor and the NFL All-Decade Teams for both the 1990s and the 2000s. He finished with the 49ers (2006-2007). He wore #71.

22. The 2014 Cowboys were beaten by the _____ in the divisional round by a score of 26-21. In that game we found out at the goal line that "a catch" is different from what we thought it to be.

23. Quarterback from Mississippi State (2016-2021) who was just a 4th round pick by Dallas but has made two Pro Bowls and compiled a 53-32 record as a starter. He is already #5 all-time for Dallas in scoring passes (143) and #4 in passing yardage (22,083). He wears #4.

24. Dallas head coach (2010-2019) whose 10 teams finished above .500 just 5 times. The Cowboys won the NFC East 3 times in his tenure but many wondered how he kept his job for so long.

25. Running back from Minnesota (2005-2010) who was a 4th round pick by Dallas and a 2007 Pro Bowler. His 47 rushing touchdowns are #4 all-time for the Cowboys and his 4,358 rushing yards are #8. His dad had also been a running back at Minnesota and a 2nd round pick by the Jets (1982-1988). He wore #24.

31. Linebacker from Appalachian State (1997-2004) who was a 3rd round pick by the Cowboys. He made the NFL All-Rookie Team and was a 3-time Pro Bowler. His streak of 7 straight seasons with 100+ tackles is a team record and no Cowboy has more than his 4 defensive touchdowns. He wore #52.

34. Undrafted kicker from Louisiana Tech (1994-1996) who was a 1996 Super Bowl Champion and his 81 field goals are #3 all-time for Dallas. He tied the NFL record with 7 field goals in a 1996 game and he was the first Cowboy kicker to score 100 points in 3 straight seasons. He wore #18.

36. Linebacker/defensive end from Troy State (2005-2013) who was a 1st round pick by Dallas and a 7-time Pro Bowler. He is the all-time franchise sacks leader (117) and is a member of the NFL 2000s All-Decade Team. With Denver (2014-2016) he made two more Pro Bowls.

37. Wide-out from Colorado State (2018-2021) who was a 3rd round pick by the Cowboys. He had 1,100+ receiving yards in 2019 and 800+ in 2020 but just 400+ in an injury-marred 2021. He wears #13.

38. Undrafted quarterback from Eastern Illinois (2003-2016) who was a 4-time Pro Bowler and is the all-time franchise leader in passing yardage (34,183) and touchdown passes (248). He had a 78-49 record as a starter but his lack of postseason success is an enduring stigma. He wore #9.

40. Defensive back from Arizona State (1992-2003) who was a 2nd round pick, a 5-time Pro Bowler and a 3-time Super Bowl Champion (1993, 1994 and 1996). He played only for Dallas and is a member of the Cowboy Ring of Honor. He is the all-time franchise leader in solo tackles (827). He wore #28.

43. Undrafted defensive back from Grambling (1981-1989) who led the NFL in interceptions 3 times. He was a 1978 Super Bowl Champion and his 44 career interceptions are #2 in team history. Sadly, it has been "The Catch" by Dwight Clark of the 49ers in 1982 that has immortalized him. He wore #24.

44. Hall of Fame linebacker defensive end from James Madison (1992-1996) who had been a 4th round pick by the 49ers (1986-1991 and 1998-1999). He was a 5-time Super Bowl Champion, twice with San Francisco (1989 and 1990) and 3 times with Dallas (1993, 1994 and 1996). He wore #94.

47. Center from Pittsburgh (1989-1994 and 1999-2001) who was a 3rd round pick by Dallas, a 3-time Pro Bowler and a 2-time Super Bowl Champion (1993 and 1994). He is a member of the NFL 1990s All-Decade Team and has long been an outspoken critic of punitive US marijuana laws. He wore #53.

DALLAS COWBOYS

49. Undrafted defensive back from Tennessee (1983-1997) who was a 3-time Super Bowl Champion for the Cowboys (1993, 1994 and 1996). He was known as a big hitter, both from scrimmage and on special teams. He played in 217 games, all with Dallas and wore #40.

51. Hall of Fame Dallas head coach (2003-2006) whose teams compiled a cumulative 34-20 record, with no playoff wins. As head coach of the Giants, he was a 2-time Super Bowl Champion (1978 and 1991). He led the Patriots to the 1997 Super Bowl and also went 29-19 with the Jets (1997-1999).

54. Hall of Fame wide-out from Miami (1988-1999) who was a 1st round pick and only played for Dallas. He was a 5-time Pro Bowler and a 3-time Super Bowl Champion (1993, 1994 and 1996). He was the first Cowboy to reach 700 catches and 10,000 receiving yards. He now does analyst work for ESPN. He wore #88.

55. Defensive end from Boise State (2014-2021) who was a 2nd round pick and has only played for Dallas so far. He is a 2-time Pro Bowler and has recorded 49 sacks and forced 17 fumbles. He has earned the nickname "Tank" and wears #90.

58. Center/guard from Colorado (2002-2010) who was a 2nd round pick and 5- time Pro Bowler for Dallas. He was the first Cowboy rookie to start at center in a season opener and started every game (2008-2010). He finished up with the Ravens (2011) and Raiders (2013). He wore #65.

60. Linebacker from UCLA (1988-1993) who was a 2nd round pick by Dallas and a 2-time Super Bowl Champion (1993 and 1994). With the 49ers (1994-2000), he became the only player to be a Super Bowl Champion in 3 straight seasons (1995). His dad was a prominent heavyweight boxer. He wore #51.

61. Wide-out from Oklahoma State (2010-2017) who was a 1st round pick and a 3-time Pro Bowler for Dallas, with 1,200+ receiving yards in 3 straight seasons. With the Saints in 2018 he tore an Achilles but played in 6 games for the Ravens in 2020. His 73 touchdown catches are #1 in Cowboy history. He wore #88.

62. 335-pound guard from Florida A&M (1986-1998) who came to Dallas after two years in the USFL. With the Cowboys, he was a 6-time Pro Bowler and a 3-time Super Bowl Champion (1993, 1994 and 1996). In retirement he served a 30-month term in federal prison for drug trafficking. He wore #73.

66. The first name of the player referred to in 28 ACROSS.

69. The _____ beat the 2018 Cowboys in the divisional round by a score of 30-22.

DALLAS COWBOYS

DALLAS COWBOYS

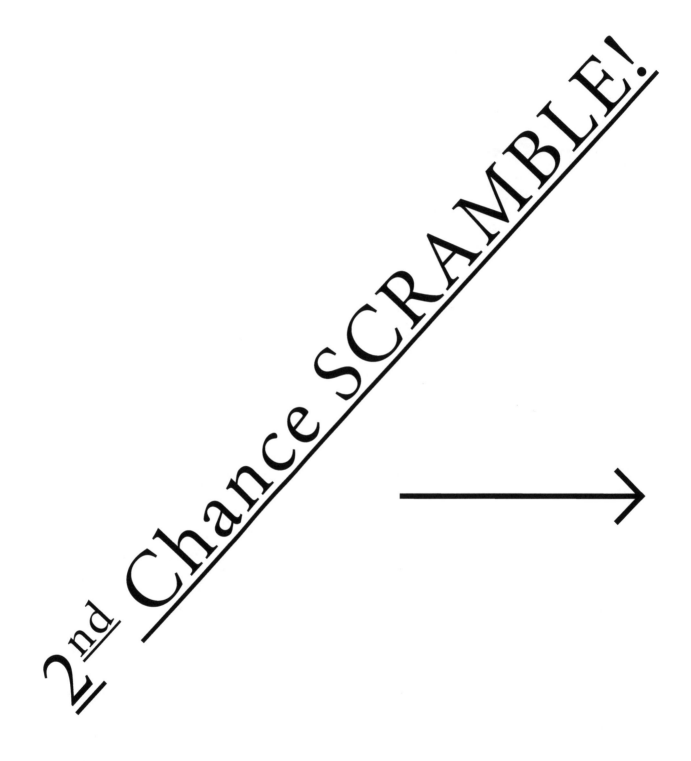

2nd Chance SCRAMBLE!

DALLAS COWBOYS

ACROSS		DOWN	
1. NEWITT	_ _ _ _ _ _	2. TNERRU	_ _ _ _ _ _
6. ILTTLEO	_ _ _ _ _ _ _	3. ESLIL	_ _ _ _ _
8. BMAL	_ _ _ _	4. ZDE	_ _ _
14. EEL	_ _ _	5. JSEON	_ _ _ _ _
15. IRNTAM	_ _ _ _ _ _	7. ASWLMIIL	_ _ _ _ _ _ _ _
16. UTAINS	_ _ _ _ _ _	9. AYLBSEE	_ _ _ _ _ _ _
17. COEL	_ _ _ _	10. GGSDI	_ _ _ _ _
18. GYEIAL	_ _ _ _ _ _	11. ILAEBY	_ _ _ _ _ _
19. ANSE	_ _ _ _	12. GAENR	_ _ _ _ _
20. AADSM	_ _ _ _ _	13. LNSIO	_ _ _ _ _
26. DNA	_ _ _	21. AELLN	_ _ _ _ _
27. NLIUEERZ	_ _ _ _ _ _ _ _	22. PCSAEKR	_ _ _ _ _ _ _
28. VASID	_ _ _ _ _	23. TECSOTPR	_ _ _ _ _ _ _ _
30. NMOIAR	_ _ _ _ _ _	24. GRTRETA	_ _ _ _ _ _ _
32. KVCOEAN	_ _ _ _ _ _ _	25. ERBBRA	_ _ _ _ _ _
33. LRTETBO	_ _ _ _ _ _ _	31. COLKAYE	_ _ _ _ _ _ _
35. TJTE	_ _ _ _	34. INLBOO	_ _ _ _ _ _
39. MNNEAW	_ _ _ _ _ _	36. ERWA	_ _ _ _
41. EGAE	_ _ _ _	37. UALLGP	_ _ _ _ _ _
42. SONJNOH	_ _ _ _ _ _ _	38. OMOR	_ _ _ _
45. EOLDSBE	_ _ _ _ _ _ _	40. DSOOWNO	_ _ _ _ _ _ _
46. SSAPRON	_ _ _ _ _ _ _	43. WSLAL	_ _ _ _ _
50. IPPISLLH	_ _ _ _ _ _ _ _	44. YEHLA	_ _ _ _ _
52. AGLEE	_ _ _ _ _	47. TOKSNEIPS	_ _ _ _ _ _ _ _ _
52. REIK	_ _ _ _	49. TEABS	_ _ _ _ _
53. AOMPC	_ _ _ _ _	51. PREALSLC	_ _ _ _ _ _ _ _
56. WSETZIR	_ _ _ _ _ _ _	54. VNIRI	_ _ _ _ _
57. ROOPCE	_ _ _ _ _ _	55. NELECWAR	_ _ _ _ _ _ _ _
59. LASMII	_ _ _ _ _ _	58. EODGUR	_ _ _ _ _ _
63. ARUMYR	_ _ _ _ _ _	60. ONRONT	_ _ _ _ _ _
64. OYRT	_ _ _ _	61. BARNTY	_ _ _ _ _ _
65. JSOOHNN	_ _ _ _ _ _ _	62. NWEONT	_ _ _ _ _ _
68. AINAMK	_ _ _ _ _ _	66. MAIRA	_ _ _ _ _
70. ADLRNMAY	_ _ _ _ _ _ _ _	69. KNE	_ _ _
71. SENOW	_ _ _ _ _		

XLIII

WASHINGTON FOOTBALL TEAM

ACROSS

1. Linebacker from Penn State (2000-2005) who was a 1st round pick and taken 2nd overall by Washington. He was a 3-time Pro Bowler and is among the "80 Greatest Redskins". His last 2 years in Washington were marred by injuries, problems with his agent and conflicts with the coaching staff. He wore #56.

3. Undrafted linebacker from John Carroll (2007-2013) who had earlier been a 2000 Super Bowl Champion with the Rams (1998-2001). He was a 4-time Pro Bowler with Washington and is among "The 80 Greatest Redskins". He holds the NFL record for most consecutive starts by a linebacker with 215. He wore #59.

6. Offensive tackle from Ohio State (1988-1995) who had been a 1st round pick by the Chargers (1985-1987). For Washington he was a 2-time Pro Bowler and a 1992 Super Bowl Champion. He is among "The 80 Greatest Redskins" and was one of "The Hogs", along with the players referred to in 25 DOWN and 33 DOWN. He wore #79.

9. Tiny receiver from James Madison (1985-1992) who was a 2nd round pick and came to Washington after 2 years in the USFL. He was a 4-time Pro Bowler and 2-time Super Bowl Champion for the Redskins (1988 & 1992). He is among "The 80 Greatest Redskins" and is a member of the Redskins Ring of Fame. He wore #84.

12. Linebacker from Purdue (2011-2019) who was a 1st round pick and has only played for the Redskins. He has made 4 Pro Bowls to date. His 26 forced fumbles are the most in the team's recorded history and his 90 career sacks are the 2nd most (1 behind Dexter Manley). He started every game in his first 8 seasons. He wears #91.

13. Running back from Iowa (2002-2009) who was a 2nd round pick by Washington. He was mainly a back-up but he did have 1,100 rushing yards in 2006 when the player referred to in 15 DOWN was hurt. That year had a 171-yard game vs. the Eagles and he is the only Redskin with consecutive 150-yard games. He wore #46.

14. The first name of the player referred to in 36 ACROSS.

15. The first name of the coach referred to in 18 ACROSS.

17. Defensive back from Miami (2004-2097) who was a 1st round pick and taken 5th overall by Washington. He was a 2-time Pro Bowler and is a member of the Redskins Ring of Honor. He played only with Washington and his short career was marred by legal issues. He was killed in a home invasion by burglars in 2007. He wore #21.

20. Offensive tackle from Alabama (2000-2009) who was a 1st round pick and taken 3rd overall by Washington. He played only for the Redskins and was a 6-time Pro Bowler. He is among "The 80 Greatest Redskins". He started every game in 6 of his 10 seasons and averaged 14 starts per year for his career. He wore #60.

21. The first name of the player referred to in 29 ACROSS.

23. Defensive back from Virginia Tech (2008-2017) who had been a 1st round pick by Atlanta (2004-2007) for whom he was a 2-time Pro Bowler. He was a 2010 Pro Bowler for Washington, the year he tied the NFL record with a 4-interception game. He had 23 of his career 43 interceptions with Washington. He wore #23.

26. Running back from East Carolina (1989-1993) who had been a 10th round pick by Cleveland (1984-1988). He was a 2-time Pro Bowler and a 1992 Super Bowl Champion for Washington and he is among "The 80 Greatest Redskins". His 3,950 career rushing yards are the 8th most in team history. He wore #21.

27. Running back from Oklahoma (2018-2019) who had been a 1st round pick and taken 7th overall by Minnesota (2007-2016), for whom he was a 7-time Pro Bowler and the 2012 NFL MVP. He had 1,000 rushing yards for Washington in 2018 and his 14,216 career rushing yards are 5th most in NFL history. He wears #26.

28. Quarterback from Washington State (1986-1993) who was a just a 6th round pick by Washington

XLIV

but still was a 2-time Pro Bowler and 2-time Super Bowl Champion (1988 & 1992). He only played in the 1992 game and he was the game MVP that day. He is among "The 80 Greatest Redskins" and he wore #11.

29. The first name of the player referred to in 28 ACROSS.

30. The first name used by the player referred to in 22 ACROSS.

31. Heisman-winning quarterback from Baylor (2012-2015) who was a 1st round pick by the Redskins and taken 2nd overall. He was the NFL Offensive Rookie of the Year and a 2012 Pro Bowler. Knee injuries suffered late in that season, however, ruined a career that seemed to have some much promise. He wore #10.

34. Redskins head coach (1981-1992 & 2004-2007) whose teams won 3 Super Bowls (1983, 1988 & 1992). His 171 wins (including the post-season) are the most in franchise history. He spent the 12 years between his 2 coaching tours on his new career as an owner in drag racing. Maybe he should not have come back.

36. Receiver from Florida State (2003-2004) who had been a 3rd round pick by the Jets (2000-2002). He was a 2003 Pro Bowler with Washington when he had 1,200 receiving yards. He had 900 yards in 2004 and then went back to the Jets (2005-2008). His first name is unique and hard to spell and pronounce. He wore #80.

39. Speedy, 5'10" receiver from Miami (2005-2014) who had been a 1st round pick by the Jets (2001-2004). He was a 2005 Pro Bowler for the Redskins and had 3 years with 1,000 receiving yards for Washington. His 581 catches are the 3rd most in franchise history. He wore #89.

40. The first name of the coach referred to in 9 DOWN.

42. Undrafted kicker from Florida State (2009-2011) whose career field goals are the 7th most in Redskins history. He moved on to the Panthers (2012-2017) and helped them make it to the 2016

Super Bowl. His 151 field goals put him at #2 on the all-time list for that franchise. He wore #4.

43. Hall of Fame defensive back from Georgia (1999-2003) who was a 1st round pick and 4-time Pro Bowler for the Redskins. He was dealt to Denver (2004-2013) and went on to make 8 more Pro Bowls. He had 52 career interceptions, 18 with Washington. His real first name is Roland. He wore #24.

45. Undrafted punter from Wisconsin-Whitewater (1995-1999) who was a 3-time Pro Bowler for Washington. Traded after a dispute with ownership, he went on to play 11more years with 5 other teams. He wore #1.

47. Heisman-winning and San Diego high school product from Utah (2018-2019) who was a 1st round pick by the 49ers (2005-2012). He went on to be a 3-time Pro Bowler for the Chiefs (2013-2017). With Washington, he suffered a gruesome broken leg in Week 10 of 2018 that has put his career in doubt. He wore #11.

48. The first name of the player referred to in 19 ACROSS.

49. The first name used by the player referred to in 13 DOWN.

52. Washington owner (2014-2019) under whose leadership the team has gone just 142-193-1. Despite his extensive philanthropic efforts, he is easily among the least popular NFL owners.

54. Quarterback from Indiana (1997-1998) who had been an 8th round pick by the Chargers. He threw just one pass in 1997 but played well for a bad Washington team in 1998. He went on to become a Super Bowl Champ in 2000 with the Rams as a back-up to Warner. He then was a 3-time Pro Bowler for the Chiefs. He wore #10.

55. Quarterback from Grambling (1986-1989) who had been a 1st round pick by the Buccaneers (1978-1982). He came to Washington after 2 years in the USFL. He was the MVP of the 1988 Super Bowl (a 42-10 thrashing of Denver) and thus

XLV

became the first black quarterback to win a Super Bowl. He wore #17.

57. The first name of the player referred to in 28 DOWN.

59. The first name of the player referred to in 37 ACROSS.

60. Quarterback from Michigan State (2012-2017) who was a 4th round pick and a 2016 Pro Bowler for Washington. He went on to sign a huge contract with the Vikings (2018-2019) and was a 2019 Pro Bowler. His 16,000 passing yards are the 4th most in Redskins history. He wore #12 and #8.

63. Kicker from Bowling Green (2006-2009) who came to Washington from Dallas (2005-2006). His 81 field goals are the 4th most in Redskins history. He was released in December 2009 after missing a short field goal in an overtime loss to the Saints. He went on to kick 124 field goals for the Steelers (2010-2015). He wore #6.

65. Often-injured quarterback from Florida (2010-2011) who had been a 1st round pick by the Bears (2003-2008). Somehow he led Chicago to the 2007 Super Bowl but with Washington he went just 6-10 as a starter. He had more career interceptions than touchdown passes. He wore #8.

67. Undrafted punter from Oklahoma (2014-2019) who was a 2019 Pro Bowler and has only played for Washington to date. In 2016, the team signed him to a 5-year contract extension. His 46.8 yard per punt average is the highest in franchise history, a yard and a half better per kick than #2 Sammy Baugh. He wears #5.

68. The first name of the player referred to in 25 Down.

69. The first name of the player referred to in 1 DOWN.

DOWN

1. Running back from Clemson (1995-1998) who had been a 9th round pick by Minnesota (1991-1994), for whom he had 2 years with 1,000 yards rushing. He had 2 more 1,000-yard seasons with the Redskins and he led the NFL with 21 rushing

touchdowns in 1996. He is among "The 80 Greatest Redskins". He wore #21.

2. Nigerian linebacker from Texas (2009-2014) who was a 1st round pick and 3-time Pro Bowler for the Redskins. He had 11 sacks in 2009, 10 in 2013, and 40 total for Washington. With the Titans (2015-2018) he made another Pro Bowl in 2016. He wore #98.

4. 5'11, 180-pound receiver from Fresno State (1994-1998) who had been a 2nd round pick by the Rams (1983-1993), for whom he had 4 seasons with 1,000 receiving yards and was a 3-time Pro Bowler. With the Redskins he had 3 more 1,000-yard seasons. He had 13,000 career receiving yards and 65 scores. He wore #85.

5. Undrafted kicker from Wisconsin (2003-2006) who had earlier played for the Jets (1997-2002), for whom his 149 field goals are 4th in team history. With the Redskins, he had 54 field goals, 8th most in franchise history. He was known as an eager tackler on kickoffs and was often injured. He wore #10.

7. Tight end from Utah State (2004-2012) who was a 3rd round pick and a 2-time Pro Bowler for Washington. He only played for the Redskins and his 429 career catches are the 5th most in team history. He started every game in 5 seasons, including 4 years in a row (2005-2008). He went on to do some radio work for the team. He-wore #47.

8. Running back from Notre Dame (1993-19-95) who was a 2nd round pick by the Redskins and had 1,000 rushing yards as a rookie. The arrival of the player referred to in 1 DOWN cut his playing time. After a forgettable year with the Buccaneers in 1996, he retired at age 25. He is now an administrator at Notre Dame. He wore #40.

10. Undrafted quarterback from Houston (2019) who first played sparingly with the Texans and Rams (2012-2016) before emerging to lead the 2017 Vikings to the NFC Title Game. With Denver in 2018 he went 6-10 as a starter and then a disappointing 1-6 with the 2019 Redskins. He's with the Browns in 2020. He wore #8.

WASHINGTON FOOTBALL TEAM

11. Running back/returner from Louisiana-Lafayette (1990-1999) who was a 5th round pick a 1992 Super Bowl Champion and a 1995 Pro Bowler. He is the all-time NFL leader in kickoff return yardage. He is also among "The 80 Greatest Redskins" and is a member of the Redskins Ring of Honor. He wore #30.

16. Receiver from Ohio State (2019) who was a 3rd round pick and one of the bright spots in Washington's dismal 3-13 season with 58 catches for 919 yards plus 7 touchdown catches. He wears #17.

17. Redskins head coach (1994-2000) who compiled a 50-61-1 record. He also went on to fail in Oakland (2004-2005), going 9-23. His Charger teams (2007-2012) went 59-43 but he did not get the most out of the team's immense talent and is not regarded as a great leader. He has been, however, a fine offensive coordinator.

18. Punter from Iowa (1993-1994) who had been a 6th round pick by Miami (1983-1992), whom he helped to reach the 1985 Super Bowl. He was a 2-time Pro Bowler for the Dolphins and he made a 3rd with Washington (1994). He was able to pound the ball without jumping. He died of a heart attack at age 43. He wore #4.

19. Hall of Fame defensive back from Texas A&M-Kingsville (1983-2002) who was a 1st round pick, a 7-time Pro Bowler and a 2-time Super Bowl Champion (1988 & 1992). He only played for Washington and is among "The 80 Greatest Redskins". His 54 career interceptions are the most in franchise history. He wore #28.

22. Quarterback from Florida State (1999-2000) who had been a 9th round pick by Minnesota (1992-1998 & 2005-2006). He was a 1999 Pro Bowler for Washington and he went on to be a 2003 Super Bowl Champion for the Buccaneers. For the Redskins he went 17-10 as a starter. He wore #14.

24. Kicker from Minnesota (1988-1994) who was a 2nd round pick, a 1991 Pro Bowler and a 1992 Super Bowl Champion for Washington. He went on to play for the Saints (1995) and Rams (1996). His 175 field goals are the 2nd most in team

history. He went by a nickname but his real first name is John. He wore #8.

25. Kicker from Florida State (2015-2019) who had been a 6th round pick by Buffalo (2013). His 34 field goals in 2016 are the most in Washington history and his 124 career field goals to date are the 3rd most on the all-time Redskins list. He wears #4.

27. Running back from Miami (2004-2010) who had been a 2nd-round pick by Denver (2002-2003). He was a 2008 Pro Bowler and is among the "80 Greatest Redskins". He had 4 seasons with 1,000 rushing yards for Washington and his 6,824 career rushing-yards are the 2nd most in franchise history. He wore #26.

32. Quarterback from Tulsa (1994-1998) who was a 7th round pick by the Redskins and a 1996 Pro Bowler. His record as a starter for the Redskins was just 19-26-1 and he is most famous for a celebratory head-butt of an unpadded wall in the Meadowlands. Bad idea. He went on to play for 6 other teams. He wore #12.

33. The first name of the player referred to in 6 DOWN.

35. Heisman-wining Redskins head coach (2002-2003) who had earlier been a huge success as a college coach at Florida. His Washington teams, however, had records of just 7-9 and 5-11. His trademark arrogance made him unpopular among his coaching peers.

37. Quarterback from Tennessee (1994-1996) who was a 1st round pick and taken 3rd overall by Washington. He was a historic bust, however. Pressed into action right away, he went just 4-9 as a starter and was traded. He went on to serve 6 years the US House of Representatives and is now a lobbyist. He wore #5.

39. Running back from Florida Atlantic (2012-2015) who was just a 6th round pick but still a 2-time Pro Bowler for Washington. He had 3 straight years with 1,000 rushing yards (2012-2014) and his 4,713 career rushing yards are 5th most in team history. He has since gone on to 3 other teams (2016-2019). He wore #46.

41. Linebacker from Florida (1988-1992) who had been a 1st round pick by Chicago (1984-1987) for whom he was a 2-time Pro Bowler and 1986 Super Bowl Champion. With Washington he was a 1992 Super Bowl Champion and a 1992 Pro Bowler. He is among "The 80 Greatest Redskins" and wore #58.

42. Haitian receiver from Mt. Union (2012-2016) who had been a 6th round pick by the Colts (2008-2011) whom he helped to reach the 2010 Super Bowl. With Washington, he led the NFL with 113 catches in 2013 and his 376 career catches are 9th most in team history. He wore #88.

44. Quarterback from Auburn (2005-2009) who was a 1st round pick by Washington. He went 20-32 as a starter for some bad Redskins teams and then moved on to the Raiders, Bears, Browns and Bengals (2010-2014). His 1,002 completions for Washington are 6th most in franchise history. He wore #17.

46. Guard from Idaho (1989-1994) who was a 10th round pick a 1991 Pro Bowler and a 1992 Super Bowl Champion for Washington. With Denver (1995-2000) he became a Super Bowl Champion two more times (1998 & 1999). After 12 seasons and 15 knee surgeries, he retired and went to work for ESPN. He wore #69.

48. Hall of Fame receiver from Syracuse (1980-1993) who was a 1st round pick by Washington. He was a 3-time Pro Bowler and a 3-time Super Bowl Champion (1983, 1988 and 1992). His 888 catches and 12,000 receiving yards are the most in franchise history and he is among "The 80 Greatest Redskins". He wore #81.

50. Quarterback from Ohio State (2019) who was a 1st round pick by Washington. He was pressed into service before he was ready and went 2-5 as a starter for a bad team. He wears #7.

51. Redskins head coach (2014-2019) who compiled a 35-50-1 record and was fired after a 0-5 start in 2019. He older brother is more famous.

52. Receiver from Texas State (1986-1993) who came to the Redskins after 2 years in the USFL. He was a 2-time Super Bowl Champion for Washington (1988 & 1?992) and he is among "The 80 Greatest Redskins". He had 2 years with 1,000 receiving yards and his 5,854 receiving yards are 6th most in team history. He wore #83.

53. The first name of the player referred to in 27 ACROSS.

55. Receiver from Colorado (1995-2001) who was a 1st round pick and taken 4th overall by Washington. He had 1,100 receiving yards in 1999 but his career was curtailed by injuries. He is infamous for injuring 2-time Pro Bowl running back Stephen Davis with a sucker punch in practice in 1997. He wore #82.

56. Defensive end from Nevada (1983-1992) who was a 3rd round pick, a 4-time Pro Bowler and a 2-time Super Bowl Champion for Washington (1987 & 1992). He is among the "80 Greatest Redskins" and is a member of the Redskins Ring of Fame. He went to win a 3rd Super Bowl with the 49ers in 1995. He wore #71.

58. The first name of the player referred to in 17 DOWN.

61. The first name of the player referred to in 5 ACROSS.

62. The first name of the player referred to in 3 ACROSS.

64. Guard from Pittsburgh (1981-1990) who was a 1st round pick, a 1988 Pro Bowler and a 2-time Super Bowl Champion for Washington (1983 & 1988). He is among the "80 Greatest Redskins". He went on be a long-time ESPN college football analyst along-side Lou Holtz (2001-2014). He wore #73.

66. The first name of the player referred to in 26 DOWN.

WASHINGTON FOOTBALL TEAM

WASHINGTON FOOTBALL TEAM

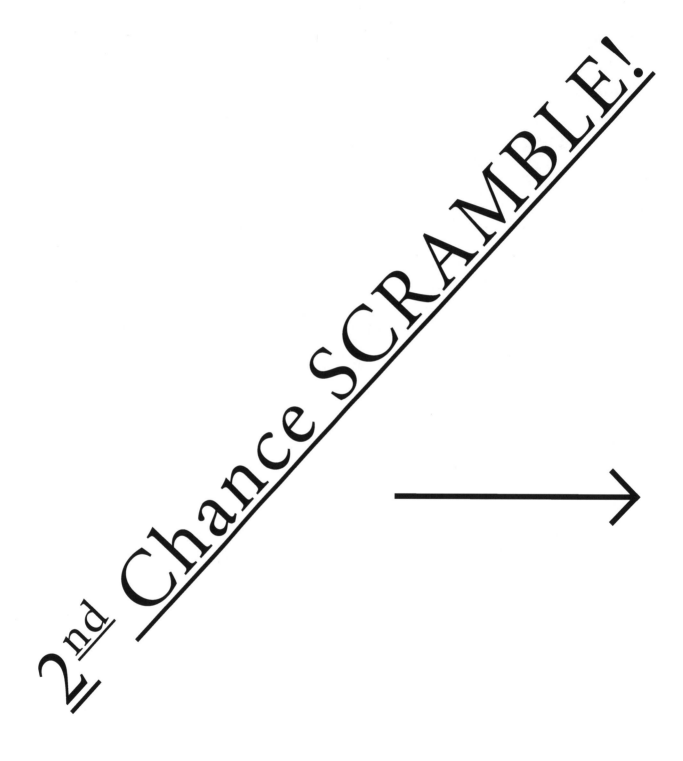

2ⁿᵈ Chance SCRAMBLE!

WASHINGTON FOOTBALL TEAM

ACROSS

#	Clue
1.	GNANOITRR ___ ___ ___ ___ ___ ___ ___ ___ ___
3.	FCTLHERE ___ ___ ___ ___ ___ ___ ___ ___
6.	LAHYCE ___ ___ ___ ___ ___ ___
9.	CKLAR ___ ___ ___ ___ ___
12.	IGAKRREN ___ ___ ___ ___ ___ ___ ___ ___
13.	ESBTT ___ ___ ___ ___ ___
14.	ELAX ___ ___ ___ ___
15.	OEJ ___ ___ ___
17.	LOTAYR ___ ___ ___ ___ ___ ___
20.	SUSLMAE ___ ___ ___ ___ ___ ___ ___
21.	RXE ___ ___ ___
23.	AHLL ___ ___ ___ ___
26.	NREYB ___ ___ ___ ___ ___
27.	ERPESNOT ___ ___ ___ ___ ___ ___ ___ ___
28.	NYRPIE ___ ___ ___ ___ ___ ___
29.	IRKK ___ ___ ___ ___
30.	MCHPA ___ ___ ___ ___ ___
31.	IFIRFNG ___ ___ ___ ___ ___ ___ ___
34.	GISBB ___ ___ ___ ___ ___
36.	OCLSE ___ ___ ___ ___ ___
39.	SSMO ___ ___ ___ ___
40.	RONV ___ ___ ___ ___
42.	OGAN ___ ___ ___ ___
43.	LYIABE ___ ___ ___ ___ ___ ___
45.	RTUK ___ ___ ___ ___
47.	HIMTS ___ ___ ___ ___ ___
48.	RKMA ___ ___ ___ ___
49.	HICP ___ ___ ___ ___
52.	NSRYED ___ ___ ___ ___ ___ ___
54.	GEENR ___ ___ ___ ___ ___
55.	LAWISMIL ___ ___ ___ ___ ___ ___ ___ ___
57.	WDNEAY ___ ___ ___ ___ ___ ___
59.	ETTNR ___ ___ ___ ___ ___
60.	UNCOSIS ___ ___ ___ ___ ___ ___ ___
63.	HSUMSAI ___ ___ ___ ___ ___ ___ ___
65.	SGSONMAR ___ ___ ___ ___ ___ ___ ___ ___
67.	WYA ___ ___ ___
68.	MRAK ___ ___ ___ ___
69.	EYRRT ___ ___ ___ ___ ___

DOWN

#	Clue
1.	LALNE ___ ___ ___ ___ ___
2.	ROPAOK ___ ___ ___ ___ ___ ___
4.	EDLRAL ___ ___ ___ ___ ___ ___
5.	LHAL ___ ___ ___ ___
7.	OEYLCO ___ ___ ___ ___ ___ ___
8.	RBKOSO ___ ___ ___ ___ ___ ___
10.	EEUNKM ___ ___ ___ ___ ___ ___
11.	IMCHLELT ___ ___ ___ ___ ___ ___ ___ ___
16.	RAMUECLN ___ ___ ___ ___ ___ ___ ___ ___
17.	NUERRT ___ ___ ___ ___ ___ ___
18.	RBYO ___ ___ ___ ___
19.	ENEGR ___ ___ ___ ___ ___
22.	SNJOONH ___ ___ ___ ___ ___ ___ ___
24.	IEHRLMOLL ___ ___ ___ ___ ___ ___ ___ ___ ___
25.	NISKHPO ___ ___ ___ ___ ___ ___ ___
27.	TPISOR ___ ___ ___ ___ ___ ___
32.	EROFTETR ___ ___ ___ ___ ___ ___ ___ ___
33.	SCAE ___ ___ ___ ___
35.	RISRPEUR ___ ___ ___ ___ ___ ___ ___ ___
37.	HRSLEU ___ ___ ___ ___ ___ ___
39.	ROISRM ___ ___ ___ ___ ___ ___
41.	MHARLSLA ___ ___ ___ ___ ___ ___ ___ ___
42.	OGCANR ___ ___ ___ ___ ___ ___
44.	PLMCALEB ___ ___ ___ ___ ___ ___ ___ ___
46.	TEELHHSRC ___ ___ ___ ___ ___ ___ ___ ___ ___
48.	KONM ___ ___ ___ ___
50.	NSKHSAI ___ ___ ___ ___ ___ ___ ___
51.	UNDRGE ___ ___ ___ ___ ___ ___
52.	SSDARNE ___ ___ ___ ___ ___ ___ ___
53.	GOUD ___ ___ ___ ___
55.	LBOOTRWSE ___ ___ ___ ___ ___ ___ ___ ___ ___
56.	AMNN ___ ___ ___ ___
58.	SGU ___ ___ ___
61.	MIJ ___ ___ ___
62.	GYRA ___ ___ ___ ___
64.	AMY ___ ___ ___
66.	RAT ___ ___ ___

LI

PHILIDELPHIA EAGLES

ACROSS

1. Quarterback from North Dakota State (2016-2019) who was a 1st round pick by the Eagles and taken 2nd overall. He was a 2017 Pro Bowler but missed the Super Bowl due to a week 14 injury. He has gone 32-24 as a starter and is already #5 alltime for the Eagles in both passing yards and scoring touchdowns. He wears #11.

4. Often-injured quarterback from Oklahoma (2015) who came to the Eagles after having been a 1st round pick by the Rams (2010-2014) and taken 1st overall. He went 18-30-1 as a starter for the Rams and then had a 7-7 record in his only year with the Eagles. He finished up with the Vikings and Cardinals. He wore #7.

7. Defensive end from North Carolina (1994-1996) who came to the Eagles after 2 years in the USFL and 8 years with the Oilers. With the Eagles he was a Pro Bowler in each of his 3 seasons, recording 13 sacks in both 1995 and 1996. He ended his career with the Chargers (1997-1998) and had 100.5 career sacks. He wore #95.

9. Fullback from Ohio State (1986-1992) who was a 1st round pick by the Eagles and is a member of the Eagle 75th Anniversary Team. Superbly versatile, his 371 catches are the 7th most all-time for the Eagles and he also rushed for 2,672 yards. He finished up with 6 seasons for the Dolphins, Patriots and Jets. He wore #41.

10. Offensive tackle from Florida State (1998-2008) who was a 1st round pick, a 3-time Pro Bowler and is a member of the Eagle 75th Anniversary Team. He started 165 out of a possible 176 regular season games for the Eagles and he helped team reach the 2005 Super Bowl. He wore #72.

12. Defensive back from Point Loma High and Arizona State (1988-1994) who was a 2nd round pick and a 5-time Pro Bowler for the Eagles. He is a member of the Eagles Hall of Fame and the Eagles 75th Anniversary Team. No Eagle has more than his 3-4 interceptions. He went on to play 7 years with the Saints and Raiders. He wore #21.

13. Hall of Fame defensive end from Tennessee (1985-1992) who was a 1st round pick by the Eagles and taken 4th overall. He was an 8-time Pro Bowler and 2-time NFL sacks leader for the Eagles. With the Packers (1993-1998) he made 5 more Pro Bowls and became a Super Bowl Champion in 1998. He wore #92.

14. The first name of the player referred to in 7 ACROSS.

17. Tight end from Cincinnati (2007-2017) who was a 5th round pick and only played for the Eagles. He became a Super Bowl Champion in his very last game and his 398 catches are the 5th most in Eagles history. He is now a personnel consultant for the Eagles. He wore #87.

19. Eagles head coach (1991-1994) who had earlier been a tight end for the Giants and Steelers (1967-1972). His Eagle teams went 37-29 in the regular season and 1-1 in the post-season. As Jets head coach, however, (1995-1996) his teams were dreadful, managing just a 4-28 record.

21. Heisman-winning running back from Georgia (1992-1994) who first played 2 years in the USFL and then went to Dallas (1986-1989), where he was a 2-time Pro Bowler. He was a disappointment with the Vikings (1989-1991) then had 1,070 rushing yards for the Eagles in 1992. Twp less productive seasons ensued. He wore #34.

22. Back-up quarterback who had been a huge star at USC but was only a 4th round pick by the Eagles (2013-2014). He appeared in just 4 games for the Eagles then went to the Bears (2016) for whom he went 1-5 as a starter. He didn't play at all in 2017 and then managed to appear in 10 games for the Bills (2018-2019). He wore #2.

24. The first name of the player referred to in 14 DOWN.

26. The first name of the player referred to in 28 ACROSS.

28. Running back from South Carolina (1997-2003) who was a 3rd round pick by the Eagles. He had 2 years with 1,000 rushing yards for the Eagles (1999 & 2002) and his 4,807 career rushing yards are 5th

most in team history. He has been on the Eagle coaching staff in varying capacities since 2011. He wore #22.

29. The first name of the player referred to in 36 ACROSS.

30. Randall Cunningham played college football at _____.

31. The first name of the player referred to in 32 ACROSS.

32. Undrafted offensive tackle from Arkansas (2009-2019) who began with the Bills (2004-2008) for whom he was a 2-time Pro Bowler. He went on to make 7 more Pro Bowls with the Eagles and he became a Super Bowl Champion in 2018. He has made 140 starts for the Eagles, including every game in 4 seasons. He wears #71.

34. Running back/kick returner from Kansas State (2014-2019) who had been a 4th round pick by the Chargers (2005-2010). He moved on to the Saints (2011-2013) before becoming a 3-time Pro Bowler with the Eagles. He missed the 2018 Super Bowl due to injury. He had 3,500 career rushing yards and 500 catches. He wore #43.

36. Receiver from Utah State (2007-2009) who had been a 3rd round pick by the Rams (2003-2006). He had a career year for the Eagles in 2007 with 77 catches for 1,100 yards. He had 4.35 speed in the 40-yard dash and scored a nearly unprecedented 48 out of 50 on the Wonderlic Intelligence Test. He wore #80.

38. The first name of the player referred to in 29 ACROSS.

40. Running back from Pittsburgh (2009-2014) who was a 2nd round pick and 3-time Pro Bowler for the Eagles. He is the all-time Eagles leader with 6,792 rushing yards. He went on to make 3 more Pro Bowls with the Bills (2015-2018) and then became a Super Bowl Champion with the Chiefs as a part-timer (2020). He wore #25.

41. Eagles head coach (2013-2015) who came to the Eagles after being a big success at Oregon (2009-2012). His Eagles teams went 10-6, 10-6 and then 6-10. He went on to the 49ers (2016) and the year

was a 2-14 disaster. His tenure at UCLA (2018-2019) has been awful to date with season records of 3-9 and 4-8.

43. The first name of the player referred to in 3 ACROSS.

44. The first name of the player referred to in 30 ACROSS.

46. Hall of Fame, diva receiver from Tennessee-Chattanooga (2004-2005) who had been a 3rd round pick by the 49ers (1996-2003). He helped the Eagles reach the 2005 Super Bowl before going on to be a star in Dallas (2006-2008). His off-putting, attention-craving personality delayed his Canton induction. He wore #81.

48. Linebacker and special teams whiz from Michigan State (1998-2004) who was a 5th round pick and a 2004 Pro Bowler. He helped the Eagles reach the 2005 Super Bowl before moving on to Atlanta (2005-2006). He has since gone on to a long career in local sports radio in Philadelphia. He wore #58.

50. Hall of Fame defensive back from Clemson (1996-2008) who was a 2nd round pick and 7-time Pro Bowler for the Eagles. He helped the team reach the 2005 Super Bowl and is a member of both the Eagles Hall of Fame and the NFL 2000s All-Decade Team. No Eagle has more than his 34 interceptions. He wore #20.

51. The first name of the player referred to in 16 ACROSS.

56. Aptly-named receiver from North Carolina State (1982-1990) who was a 1st round pick and a 5-time Pro Bowler. He only played for the Eagles and is a member of the team's Hall of Fame. He had 3 straight years with 1,000 receiving yards and his 6,464 career receiving yards are the 3rd most in franchise history. He wore #82.

58. South African kicker from Syracuse (1995-1996) who had earlier played for the Steelers (1982-1994) and is the all-time field goal leader for that franchise. With the Vikings in 1998, he made all 35 field goal tries but missed a clinching kick in the NFC Title Game. He made 4 Pro Bowls and his 538 field goals are 3rd all-time. He wore #1.

60. Defensive end from Cincinnati (2005-2014) who was a 5th round pick by the Eagles and a 2-time Pro Bowler. His 85.5 sacks are the 2nd most in franchise history and he started 139 out of a possible 160 regular season games for the Eagles. He went on to finish up with the Colts (2015-2016). He wore #58.

62. Undrafted defensive back from Cheyney (1984-1993) who is a member of the Eagles 75th Anniversary Team. He led the team in tackles 4 times and was a frequently-fined, ferocious hitter. He finished up with the Cardinals (1994-1995). He committed suicide with a gunshot to the head at age 44. He wore #20.

64. Defensive end from Cincinnati (2013-2016) who had been a 2nd round pick by the Texans (2009-2012). He was a 2014 Pro Bowler for the Eagles when he had 14.5 sacks. He started every game in his 4 seasons with the Eagles. After playing with the Rams (2017) and Giants (2018) he became an Eagles executive. He wore #98.

65. Defensive back from SMU (1983-1993) who was a 2nd round pick and a 1986 Pro Bowler. He and the playe referred to in 31 ACROSS made a terrific tandem at safety for 8 years (1986-1993). He played only with the Eagles and his 30 career interceptions are the 5th most in franchise history. He wore #48.

66. Quarterback from Syracuse (1999-2009) who was a 1st round pick and taken 2nd overall by the Eagles. He was a 6-time Pro Bowler who led the Eagles to the 2005 Super Bowl and he is a member of the Eagles Hall of Fame. He went 92-49-1 as a starter then finished with 2 awful seasons with the Redskins and Vikings. He wore #5.

67. The first name of the coach referred to in 28 DOWN.

DOWN

1. Running back from Villanova (2002-2009) who was a 3rd round pick and 2-time Pro Bowler for the Eagles. He helped the team reach the 2005 Super Bowl and is a member of the Eagles Hall of fame. He had 2 years with 1,000+ rushing yards and his 5,995 career rushing yards are the 4th most in team history. He wore #36.

2. Defensive back from Notre Dame (19-95-2003) who was a 2nd round pick and a 2002 Pro Bowler for the Eagles. He made 109 starts for Philadelphia with 19 interceptions and 11 fumble recoveries. He finished with Seattle (2004). He wore #21.

3. Tight end from Stanford (2013-2019) who was a 2nd round pick and has played only for the Eagles. He has made 3 Pro Bowls to date. He caught the winning touchdown pass in the 2018 Super Bowl and his 525 career catches are the most in franchise history. He wears #86.

4. Defensive tackle from Miami (1987-1991) who was a 1st round pick and taken 9th overall by the Eagles. He was a 2-time Pro Bowler and only played for the Eagles. He is a member of the team's Hall of Fame and his #99 has been retired. He died at age 27 with his nephew when he crashed his Corvette at high speed.

5. Heisman-winning quarter back from BYU (1996-1997) who came to the Eagles after having been a 9th round pick by Green Bay (1992-1995). He led the Eagles in passing in 1996 and went 7-4 as a starter but went just 2-5 in 1997. His younger brother was a back-up quarterback for the Eagles (1998-2006). He wore #14.

6. Receiver from Nebraska (1996-1998) who had been a 1st round pick by the Patriots and taken 1st overall (1984-1992). He was a 2-time Pro Bowler for the Eagles, with 1,000+ receiving yards in each of those seasons. Legal issues have clouded much of his life. He wore #80.

7. Quarterback from Arizona (2012-2014 & 2017-2018) who was a 3rd round pick and a 2013 Pro Bowler for the Eagles. He became a Super Bowl Champion in 2018 and was the game's MVP. 2019 was a lost year for him in Jacksonville but he is now healthy again and has signed with the Bears for 2020. He wore #9.

8. Undrafted tight-end from BYU (1997-1998 & 2000-2005) who was a 3-time Pro Bowler-with the Eagles. He caught 2 touchdown passes in the 2004 NFL Championship Game. Between his 2 tours with the Eagles he became a Super Bowl Champion with the Rams in 2000. He wore #89.

11. Quarterback from Virginia Tech (2009-2013) who had been a 1st round pick and taken 1st overall by Atlanta (2001-2008), for whom he was 3-time Pro Bowler. With the Eagles he was a 200 Pro Bowler. A electric talent, no NFL quarterback has matched his 6,000 career rushing yards. He wore #7.

15. Offensive lineman from Arkansas (2004-2009) who was a 1st round pick by the Eagles and a 2-time Pro Bowler. He helped the team reach the 2005 Super Bowl and he is a member of the Eagles 75 Anniversary Team. From 2005-2007, he started in 47 out of a possible 48 games. He wore #73.

16. Defensive back from Ohio State (2014-2019) who had been a 1st round pick by the Saints (2009-2013), for whom he was a 2010 Super Bowl Champion. He was a 3-time Pro Bowler for the Eagles and was again a Super Bowl Champion in 2018. He signed with the Saints for 2020. He wore #27.

18. Receiver from Cal (2008-2013 & 2019) who was a 2nd round pick by the Eagles and a 3-time Pro Bowler. He had 3 seasons with 1,000+ receiving yards for the Eagles and then 2 more with the Redskins in 2014 and 2016. He spent 2017-2018 with Tampa and his 2019 season with the Eagles was injury-marred. He wears #11.

20. Linebacker from Stephen F. Austin (1998-2001, 2001-2004 & 2009) who was a 3rd round pick an 4-time Pro Bowler for the Eagles. He helped the team reach the 2005 Super Bowl. He spent 2002-2003 with Washington and 2007 with Tampa Bay. He is a member of the Eagles Hall of Fame. He wore #54.

22. Guard from Miami of Ohio (2016-20 9) who had been a 3rd round pick by the Texans (2012-2015). With the Eagles, he has made 3 straight Pro Bowls to date (2017-2019), starting in all 48

regular season games. He became a Super Bowl Champion in 2 018. He wears #79.

23. Undrafted kicker from Louisville (1999-2010) who was a 5-time Pro Bowler with the Eagles. He is a member of the Eagles Hall of Fame and the NFL 2000s AllDecade Team. His 294 field goals are the most in franchise history. With the 49ers in 2011, he set the NFL record with a 44-field goal season. He wore #2.

25. Defensive back from Wisconsin (1996-2003) who had been a 1st round pick by Miami (1992-1995). With the Eagles, he was a 5-time Pro Bowler and he is a member of the Eagles Hall of Fame. His 28 career interceptions are 7th most in team history. He is now an NFL executive with multiple advanced degrees. He wore #23.

27. Long-snapper from Old Dominion (2016-2019) who had previously played for the Packers (2015) and Redskins (2016). With the Eagles he became a Super Bowl Champion in 2018 and was a 2019 Pro Bowler. He wears #45.

32. Quarterback from USC (1995-1998) who had been a 6th round pick by the Lions (1989-1993), for whom he went 21-26 as a starter. He was mainly a back-up with the Eagles but did go 9-3 as a starter in 1995 and led the team to a 58-37 rout of the Lions in a Wild Card Game. He finished up with Carolina (2002-2004). He wore #9.

33. Eagles head coach (1999-2012) who is #1 on the all-time franchise list with 130 regular season wins. He also won 10 playoff games but reached the Super Bowl just once, losing in 2005. He finally won a Super Bowl with the Chiefs in 2020.

34. Defensive end from Western Carolina (1986-1993) who was a 9th round pick and a 3-time Pro Bowler for the Eagles. He led the NFL with 19 sacks in 1992 and he is a member of the Eagles 75th Anniversary Team. His 76 career sacks are 3rd most on the all-time franchise list. He played 6 more years with 4 other teams. He wore #96.

35. Defensive end from Florida (2004-2007) who had been a 1st round pick by the Titans (1999-2003), for whom he was a 3-time Pro Bowler. He helped the Eagles reach the 2005 Super Bowl. He had 22 sacks in 39 starts for Philadelphia. He wore #93.

37. Kicker from Florida (2015-2017) who had been a 5th round pick by the Dolphins (2013-2014). With the Eagles he became a Super Bowl Champion in 2018. His 56 field goals are the 10th most in Eagles history. He played briefly with the Chargers in 2018. He wore #6.

39. Linebacker from Texas-El Paso (1986-1993) who was an 8th round pick and a 2- time Pro Bowler for the Eagles and is also a member of the Eagles 75th Anniversary Team. He made another Pro Bowl with the Cardinals (1994) and then became a Super Bowl Champion with the Broncos (1999). He wore #59.

42. Defensive back from Colorado (2002-2006) who was a 2nd round pick by the Eagles and a 2004 Pro Bowler the year he helped the team reach the 2005 Super Bowl. He started every game for the Eagles (2003-2005) and went to make 50 starts for the 49ers (2007-2010). He wore #32.

45. Famously ornery Eagles head coach (1986-1990) who had earlier risen to prominence as the defensive coordinator of the Bears team that destroyed the Patriots in the 1986 Super Bowl. His Eagles teams went 43-35-1 in the regular season but never won a playoff game.

47. Defensive tackle from Florida State (2000-2004) who was a 1st round pick and a 2003 Pro Bowler for the Eagles. He helped the team reach the 2005 Super Bowl. At 6' and 320 pounds, he was virtually immovable in the middle. He started 78 out of a possible 80 regular season games for the Eagles. He wore #90.

49. Defensive back from Central Florida (2008-2011) who had been a 4th round pick by the Patriots, for whom he was a 2-time Super Bowl Champion. With the Eagles he was a 3-time Pro Bowler who led the NFL in 2009 with 9 interceptions and the NFC with 7 in 2010. He had 51 career interceptions in 11 NFL seasons. He wore #22.

52. Linebacker from Texas A&M (1991-1999) who was a 4th round pick by the Eagles and a 2-time Pro Bowler. With the Eagles he started 129 out of a possible 144 regular season games. He finished up with Oakland (2000-2001). He excelled at both run and pass defense with 37 career sacks and 27 interceptions. He wore #51.

53. Running back from Notre Dame (1995-1997) who had been a 2nd round pick by the 49ers, for whom he was a 1995 Super Bowl Champ. He had 1,000 rushing yards in each of his 3 seasons with the Eagles. 3 more 1,000 yard seasons in Seattle made him just the 2nd player to reach that mark with 3 different teams. He wore #32.

54. The first name of the player referred to in 33 DOWN.

55. The first name of the player referred to in 21 DOWN.

57. Center from Cincinnati (2011-2019) who was a 6th round pick and has only played for the Eagles to date. He has made 3 Pro Bowls and he became a Super Bowl Champion in 2018. He has started every game over the last 5 seasons (2015-2019). His younger brother is a star with the Chiefs. He wears #62.

59. Eagles head coach (1995-1998) whose first 2 teams went 10-6 and 10-6. His last 2 teams however, went 6-9-1 and 3-13. He was hired in 1999 to be the Packers head coach and his only team went 8-8.

60. The first name of the player referred to in 1 ACROSS.

61. Undrafted kicker from Auburn (2014-2015) who set an NFL record for rookies by scoring 150 points in his only Pro Bowl season. He hit on 32 of 36 field goal tries but was hurt in 2015 and finally cut. With the Bears he displayed an uncanny knack for hitting uprights in 2018, helping the Eagles reach the Super Bowl. He wore #1.

63. The first name of the player referred to in 23 DOWN.

PHILIDELPHIA EAGLES

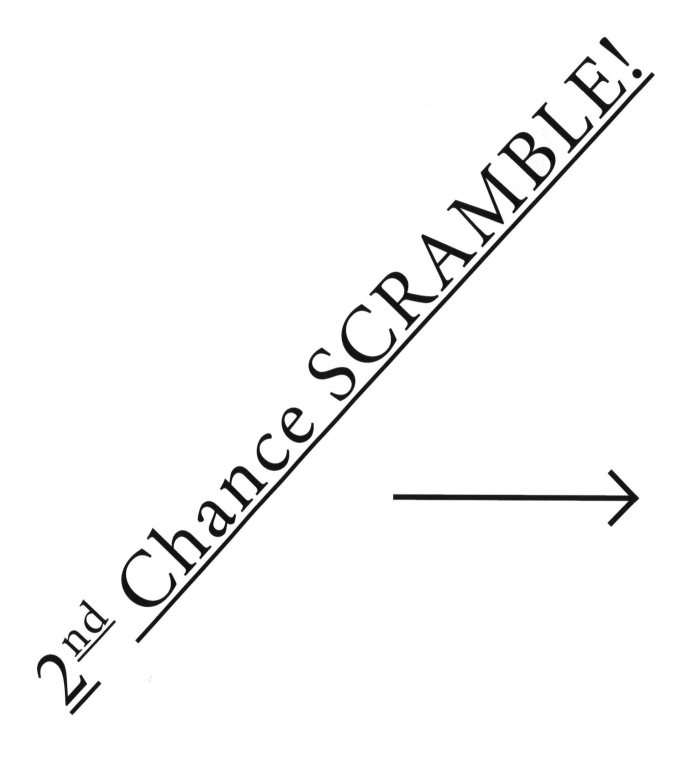

2nd Chance SCRAMBLE!

LVIII

PHILIDELPHIA EAGLES

ACROSS

1. ENZTW __ __ __ __ __
4. RDFDBAOR __ __ __ __ __ __ __ __
7. ULELFR __ __ __ __ __ __
9. ARSYB __ __ __ __ __
10. SAOTHM __ __ __ __ __ __
12. LNLEA __ __ __ __ __
13. HTWIE __ __ __ __ __
14. SMA __ __ __
17. ELKCE __ __ __ __ __
19. KOTEIT __ __ __ __ __ __
21. LWRAKE __ __ __ __ __ __
22. AYBRLKE __ __ __ __ __ __ __
24. ORTY __ __ __ __
26. KEI __ __ __
28. TASELY __ __ __ __ __ __
29. TNERT __ __ __ __ __
30. UNVL __ __ __ __
31. WES __ __ __
32. TREPES __ __ __ __ __ __
34. RPLOSSE __ __ __ __ __ __ __
36. ITRUCS __ __ __ __ __ __
38. IMEK __ __ __ __
40. COCYM __ __ __ __ __
41. EKLLY __ __ __ __ __
43. ATR __ __ __
44. GRAY __ __ __ __
46. ONWSE __ __ __ __ __
48. EREES __ __ __ __ __
50. KSNWAID __ __ __ __ __ __ __
51. TTAM __ __ __ __
56. UICKQ __ __ __ __ __
58. SANONRED __ __ __ __ __ __ __ __
60. ECLO __ __ __ __
62. TRSEAW __ __ __ __ __ __
64. WRBINA __ __ __ __ __ __
65. HINPKOS __ __ __ __ __ __ __
66. MACBNB __ __ __ __ __ __
67. RAY __ __ __

DOWN

1. EOKTRSWBO __ __ __ __ __ __ __ __ __
2. LTORYA __ __ __ __ __ __
3. RZET __ __ __ __
4. OWRBN __ __ __ __ __
5. MTERDE __ __ __ __ __ __
6. YRAFR __ __ __ __ __
7. LOFSE __ __ __ __ __
8. SLWEI __ __ __ __ __
11. CVIK __ __ __ __
15. SNAREDW __ __ __ __ __ __ __
16. IEJKNNS __ __ __ __ __ __ __
18. OCJKANS __ __ __ __ __ __ __
20. RERTTTO __ __ __ __ __ __ __
22. KOORSB __ __ __ __ __ __
23. EARSK __ __ __ __ __
25. ENCNVIT __ __ __ __ __ __ __
27. LAOVTO __ __ __ __ __ __
32. EETEP __ __ __ __ __
33. IERD __ __ __ __
34. OSNIMSM __ __ __ __ __ __ __
35. AESERK __ __ __ __ __ __
37. SIGTSUR __ __ __ __ __ __ __
39. JNREYO __ __ __ __ __ __
42. SEIWL __ __ __ __ __
45. RNAY __ __ __ __
47. SMINO __ __ __ __ __
49. ALSUME __ __ __ __ __ __
52. AOSHTM __ __ __ __ __ __
53. TTESWAR __ __ __ __ __ __ __
54. NTASAE __ __ __ __ __ __
55. BCEAL __ __ __ __ __
57. LCEEK __ __ __ __ __
59. RSHEDO __ __ __ __ __ __
60. CSANOR __ __ __ __ __ __
61. PKERYA __ __ __ __ __ __
63. ESHT __ __ __ __

LIX

SAN FRANSICSCO 49ERS

ACROSS

1. Tight end from Iowa (2017-2020) who caught only 48 balls in college and so was just a 5th round pick. With the 49ers, however, he has made 2 Pro Bowls, to date, and he set the NFL record for most receiving yards in a season by a tight end in 2018 with 1,377. He caught 85+ passes in both 2018 and 2019. He wears #85.

3. Receiver from South Carolina (2019-2020) who was a 2nd round pick. As a rookie he made a splash with 57 catches for the team that reached the Super Bowl. In 2020, however, he played in just 7 games due to injury and was limited to 33 catches. He wears #19.

7. Hall of Fame, diva receiver from Tennessee-Chattanooga (1996-2003) who was a 3rd round pick by the 49ers, for who he was a 3-time Pro Bowler and 2-time NFL leader in scoring catches. He is 2nd all-time for SF in catches, yards receiving and scoring catches. He went on to be a divisive star with two other teams. He wore #81.

10. The first name of the coach referred to in 35 ACROSS.

11. The first name of the player referred to in 4 DOWN.

12. Fullback from Nebraska (1983-1990) who was a 3rd round pick a 4-time Pro Bowler and a 2-time Super Bowl Champion for the 49ers. He had 1,900 career rushing yards and made 290 catches for SF and was also a punishing lead blocker. He then served 14 seasons as a 49er assistant coach. He wore #44.

13. The 2012 team lost to the _____ in the Super Bowl by a score of 34-31.

15. 49er head coach and GM (2005-2008) whose teams compiled an 18-37 record. Before and after his 49er tenure he was a defensive assistant coach for 25 seasons with 9 other NFL teams. His dad was the 49er head coach (1968-1975) and his teams won 3 straight NFC West division titles (1970-1972).

17. The first name of the player referred to in 6 ACROSS.

18. The first name of the player referred to in 13 DOWN.

19. Defensive back from Iowa (1991-1998) who was a 5th round pick a 4-time Pro Bowler and a 1995 Super Bowl Champion. His 31 career interceptions are #4 on the all-time 49er list. He went on to serve as assistant director of operations for the NFL and as vice-president in charge of player conduct. He wore #36.

20. 49er head coach (1997-2002) who compiled a 57-39 record, with 2 NFC West titles (1997 & 2000). He then went on to lead the Lions to 3 losing seasons (2003-2005). He has since gone on to a career as an NFL television analyst.

24. Running back from Tennessee (1999-2000) who came to the 49ers after 5 years with the Eagles (1994-1998). He had 1,000+ rushing yards in both of his years in SF and was a 2000 Pro Bowler but never duplicated these successes with any other team over his 11-year career. He wore #25.

28. Linebacker from Virginia (2008-2016) who had been a 3rd round pick by the Bengals (2006-2007). He was a 2013 Pro Bowler for the 49ers and started 91out of 96 games over 2011-2016, including every game for the 2012 team that reached the Super Bowl. He wore #55.

30. Undrafted running back from Georgia Southern (2017-2019) who led the 2018 team that went 4-12 with 814 rushing yards. He had 623 yards and a 5.1 yards per carry average for the 2019 team that reached the Super Bowl. He was dealt to Miami for 2020 but did not play due to Covid. He wore #22.

31. Undrafted quarterback from Southern Miss (2017-2020) who has been called on to make 16 starts to date for the 49ers due to injuries to Garoppolo. He has gone just 5-11 in that role but has had some big games. He wears #4.

34. Running back from Nebraska (1983-1990) who was a 2nd round pick, a 3-time Super Bowl Champion and a 4-time Pro Bowler for the 49ers. He is a member of the NFL 1980s All-Decade Team and is #3 all-time for SF in both rushing yards (7,064) and catches (508). He wore #33.

35. The first name of the coach referred to in 13 ACROSS.

38. The 2013 49ers lost the NFC Championship Game to _____ by a score of 23-17.

39. The first name of the player referred to in 22 ACROSS.

40. Tight end from Santa Clara (1987-1997) who was a 5th round pick and only played for the 49ers. He was a 4-time Pro Bowler and a 3-time Super Bowl Champion and his 417 career catches are the 6th most in team history. He wore #88 & #84.

43. Defensive back from Washington (2007-2012) who was a 4th round pick and a 2-time Pro Bowler for the 49ers. He made 64 starts for SF, including every game for the 2012 team that reached the Super Bowl. He had 14 interceptions for the 49ers before finishing with Tampa (2013-2014) and Washington (20915). He wore #38.

44. Kicker from Penn State (2017-2020) who had earlier made 276 field goals for the Bears (2005-2015). With the 49ers he led the NFL in 2017 with 39 field goals, out of just 41 attempts, and in 2018 he hit 33 out of 34! He missed 12 field goal tries over 2019-2020 but still owns an 88% success rate with SF. He wears #9.

45. The first name of the player referred to in 32 DOWN.

47. The first name of the coach referred to in 7 DOWN.

48. Running back from Notre Dame (1991-1994) who was a 2nd round pick, a 3- time Pro Bowler and a 1995 Super Bowl Champion for the 49ers. He had 1,000 rushing yards in 1992 and then had a remarkable run of 6 straight 1,000-yard seasons

with the Eagles (1995-1997) and Seahawks (1998-2000). He wore #32.

51. Left-footed kicker from Louisville (2011-2012) who had earlier made a franchise-record 294 field goals for the Eagles (1999-2010). With the 49ers he led the NFL with a career-best 44 field goals in 2011 and he made 29 for the 2012 team that made it to the Super Bowl. He wore #8.

53. 49er head coach (1989-1996) whose 1989 and 1994 teams won Super Bowls. His 108 career wins are the most in franchise history. He went on to be the head man in Carolina (1999-2001) but his team just went 16-32.

55. The first name of the player referred to in 16 ACROSS.

56. Receiver from Florida State (2013-2015) who had been a 2nd round pick by Arizona (2003-2009). He came to the 49ers after playing for the Ravens (2010-2012) and helping them beat the 2012 49ers in the Super Bowl. He had 2 years with 80+ catches and 1,000+ receiving yards for SF. He wore #81.

58. Heisman-winning quarterback from Utah (2005-2012) who was a 1st round pick by the 49ers. He was solid game manager with SF but became a 3-time Pro Bowler with the Chiefs (2013-2017). With Washington (2018-2020) he made an amazing recovery from a gruesome leg injury suffered in 2018. He wears #11.

59. Defensive tackle/end from Notre Dame (1994-2007) who was a 1st round pick and only played for the 49ers. He was a 1995 Super Bowl Champion and 4-time Pro Bowler who made 208 career starts, including every game in 9 of his 14 seasons. He is a member of the NFL 1990s All-Decade Team and wore #97.

61. The 2019 49ers beat the _____ in the NFC Championship Game by a score of 37- 20.

64. The first name of the player referred to in 14 DOWN.

65. Quarterback from San Jose State (1999-2003) who, though undrafted, became a 4-time CFL All-Star and 1998 Grey Cup Champion. With the 49ers he was a 3-time Pro Bowler and helped the team win the NFC West in 2002. He also had a Pro Bowl season with the 2007 Buccaneers. He wore #5.

66. 49er head coach (2016) whose only season was a 2-14 disaster. He had risen to prominence as the head man at Oregon (2009-2012) where his teams went 46-7. Based on that success he took the Eagles to a pair of 10-6 seasons before getting fired. At UCLA (2018-2021) he has gone just 18-25.

67. Hall of Fame receiver from Mississippi Valley State (1985-2000) who holds virtually every meaningful NFL career receiving record. He was a 13-time Pro Bowler and a 3-time Super Bowl Champion for the 49ers and wore #80.

DOWN

1. Quarterback from Nevada (2011-2016) who was a 2nd round pick and only played for the 49ers. A dangerous runner, he grew as a passer enough to lead the 2012 team to the Super Bowl but his career record as a starter was just 28-30 due to a sharp decline in team talent. His activism eventually cost his career. He wore #7.

2. Receiver from Delaware State (1987-1995) who was a 3rd round pick and a 2- time Pro Bowler. He only played for the 49ers and was a 3-time Super Bowl Champion (1989, 1990 & 1995). He caught the winning touchdown pass with just 34 seconds left to beat the Bengals in his 1st Super Bowl. He wore #82.

4. Hall of Fame quarterback from Notre Dame (1979-1992) who was a 3rd round pick a 7-time Pro Bowler and a 4-time Super Bowl Champion for the 49ers (1982, 1985, 1989 & 1990). He wore #16.

5. Hall of Fame defensive back from USC (1981-1990) who was a 1st round pick a 9- time Pro Bowler and a 4-time Super Bowl Champion for the 49ers. He was a fierce hitter, with a franchise-best 51 career interceptions. He is a member of the NFL AllDecade Teams for both the 1980s and 1990s. The team has retired his #42.

6. Linebacker from Michigan State (2000-2005) who was a 1st round pick and a 2- time Pro Bowler for the 49ers. He made 72 career starts for SF, including every game in both 2002 and 2003. He went on to be a 3-time Pro Bowler with the Seahawks (2006-2008) before finishing with the 2008 Lions. He wore #98.

8. 49er head coach (2017-2020) whose 2019 team reached the Super Bowl. His other 3 teams had losing records, largely due to injuries, especially at quarterback. He is regarded as a brilliantly creative offensive coach.

9. Linebacker from UCLA (1994-2000) who carne to the 49ers from Dallas (1988-1993), for whom he was a one-time Pro Bowler and 2-time Super Bowl Champion. With the 49ers he was a 2-time Pro Bowler and a 1995 Super Bowl Champion. He has gone on to be the Seattle defensive coordinator (2018-2020). He wore #51.

14. Running back from Purdue (2016-2020). Undrafted, he was unable to establish himself with 4 teams (2015-2016) before coming to the 49ers. He was the leading rusher for the 2019 team that made it to the Super Bowl with 772 yards. A dynamic, exciting runner, he has a career 5.6 yard average over 282 NFL carries. He wears #31.

16. The first name of the player referred to in 9 DOWN.

21. The first name of the player referred to in 1 DOWN.

22. The first name of the player referred to in 17 ACROSS.

23. Defensive tackle from Kansas 1993-1997 & 2001-2002 who was a 1st round pick, a 3-time Pro Bowler and a 1995 Super Bowl Champion for the 49ers. He was the NFL Defensive Rookie of Year and the 1997 Defensive Player of the Year. In 2020 he began a 15-year prison term. He wore #94.

25. Hall of Fame guard /tackle from Sonoma State (2006-2007) who had been a 1996 Super Bowl Champion and 10-time Pro Bowler for the Cowboys (1994-2005). He was a 2006 Pro Bowler for SF and started every game in 2007 at age 36. He is a member of the NFL All-Decade Team for both the 1990s and 2000s. He wore #71.

26. Quarterback from Michigan (1993-1996) who was an 8th round pick and a Super Bowl Champion for the 1994 team. He was mainly a back-up for the 49ers but did go 6-3 in his rare starts. With the Chiefs (1997-2000) he got more playing time and went 26-21 as a starter. He wore #18.

27. Receiver from Texas Tech (2009-2014) who was a 1st round pick by the 49ers. He had a career-best 85 catches and 1,100 receiving yards for the 2012 team that reached the Super Bowl and you may recall that un-flagged mugging he was given on 4th down at the Baltimore 7-yard line with 2:00 left. He wore #15.

29. Punter from Pittsburgh (2004-2014) who was a 6th round pick and a 3-time Pro Bowler for the 49ers. His 941 punts for the 49ers are the most in team history and he is #3 in NFL history with 1,348 punts. He has gone on to punt for the Browns (2015), Panthers (2016) and Cardinals (2017-2020). He wore #4.

32. 49er head coach (2011-2014) who compiled a 64-44 record for the 49ers and led the 2012 team to the Super Bowl. He had been an NFL quarterback for 14 seasons and then a successful head coach at Stanford (2007-2010). He has gone 49-22 to date as the head man at Michigan (2015-2020) but he has yet to beat Ohio State.

33. Linebacker/defensive end from James Madison (1986-1991 & 1998-1999) who was a 4th round pick. He also played for Dallas (1992-1996) and was a 5-time Pro Bowler and 5-time Super Bowl Champion in his 13-year career. He was the NFC Defensive Player of the Year (1990 & 1994) and had 100 career sacks. He wore #94.

36. Running back from Georgia (1997-1998 & 2001, 2003) who had been a 1st round pick by Arizona (1993-1995). With the 49ers he was a 2-time Pro Bowler who had 1,000+ rushing yards in both 1997 & 1998. He missed all of 1999-2000 due to injury but came back in 2001 with another 1,000-yard season. He wore #20.

37. Linebacker from West Chester (1994-1999) who was a 6th round pick and a 2- time Pro Bowler for the 49ers. As a rookie, he made 13 starts for the 1994 team that trashed the Chargers in the Super Bowl and he made 88 career starts for SF. He went on to start every game for the 2000 Panthers. He wore #54.

39. Defensive back from Auburn (2011-2013) who had been a 1st round pick by Washington (2005-2010). He was a 2011 Pro Bowler for the 49ers when he had 6 interceptions. He started every game in his 3 seasons in SF and helped the 2012 team make it to the Super Bowl. He wore #22.

41. Linebacker from Penn State (2010-2017) who was a 3rd round pick by the 49ers and a 3-time Pro Bowler. He started every game in 4 of his seasons in SF, including 2012 for the team that reached the Super Bowl and had 3 years with 100+ solo tackles. He wore #53.

42. Defensive tackle from Oregon (2016-2019) who was a 1st round pick and a 2018 Pro Bowler for the 49ers. He started 63 out of a possible 64 games for SF and helped the 2019 team make it to the Super Bowl. In the 2019-2020 off season he was traded to the Colts and made 14 starts for them in 2020. He wore #99.

46. Nose tackle from SMU (1984-199 2) who was a 5th round pick and only played for the 49ers, for whom he was a 3-time Super Bowl. Champion (1985, 1989 & 1990). He was also a 4-time NCAA shot put champion and an Olympic silver medalist in the 1984 Olympiad in Los Angeles. He wore #95.

49. Defensive end from Missouri (2011-2014) who was a 1st round pick by the 49ers and a 2012 Pro Bowler when he helped the team make it to the Super Bowl. He then moved on to the Raiders for 2015 but missed the next 4 seasons due to drug suspensions. He came back to make every start for Dallas in 2020. He wore #99.

50. Quarterback from Louisiana Tech (2000-2005) who was a 7th round pick by the 49ers. He was mainly a back-up on some bad teams, going 4-12 in his starting opportunities. He wore #13.

52. The 2012 team beat _____ in the NFC Championship Game by a score of 28-24.

54. Kicker from Texas (2013-2016) who had earlier made 305 field goals for the Browns (1999-2012). For the 49ers he made 99 field goals, #6 in team history, and his 441 career field goals place him at #8 on the all-time NFL list. He wore #9 & #4.

57. Left-footed kicker from San Jose State (2005-2010) who came to the 49ers after kicking for 7 other teams (1996-2004). With SF he made 129 field goals, #3 in franchise history, with an 87% success rate. He wore #6.

58. Center/guard from Samoa who played at Hawaii (1983-1997) and, despite being just an 11th round pick was a 2-time Pro Bowler and 4-time Super Bowl Champion for the 49ers. He only played for SF and started every game in 8 seasons, including 6 in a row (1988-1993). He wore #61.

60 Running back from Miami (2005-2014) who was a 3rd round pick and a 4-time Pro Bowler for the 49ers. He had 8 years in SF with 1,000+ rushing yards and he is #1 all-time for the 49ers with 11,000+ career yards. He had 1,000+ yards for the 2016 Colts and 600+ yards for the 2020 Jets at age 37! He wore #21.

62. Defensive back-from LSU (2013-2017) who was a 1st round pick and a 2013 Pro Bowler for the 49ers. He made 69 starts for SF, with 10 interceptions and then made 29 starts for Carolina (2018-2019). He was an early participant in the national anthem protests and a vocal supporter of the player referred to in 1 DOWN. He wore #35.

63. The first name of the player referred to in 3 DOWN.

SAN FRANSICSCO 49ERS

SAN FRANSICSCO 49ERS

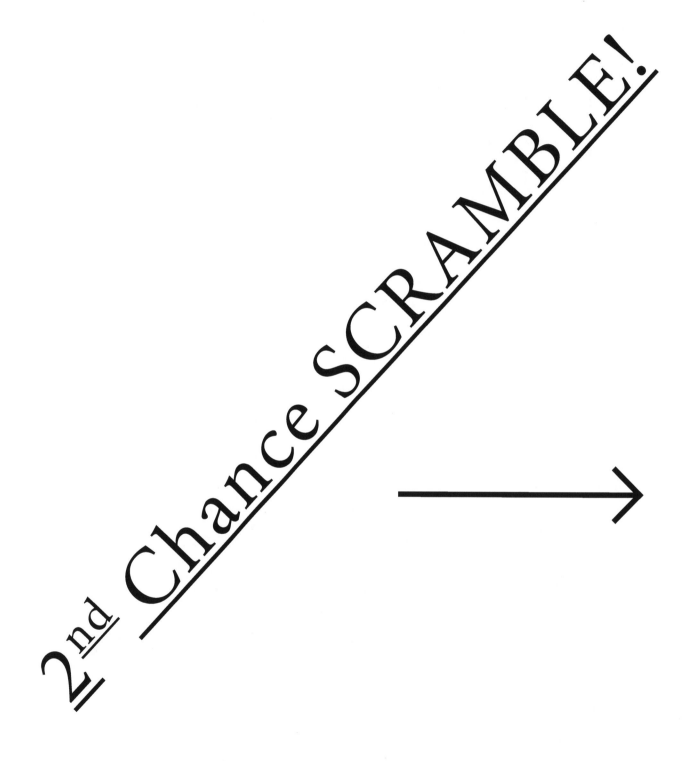

2ⁿᵈ Chance SCRAMBLE!

LXVI

SAN FRANSICSCO 49ERS

ACROSS

1. TIKETL _ _ _ _ _ _
3. SALEMU _ _ _ _ _ _
7. NOESW _ _ _ _ _
10. HIPC _ _ _ _
11. OEJ _ _ _
12. AAHMRNT _ _ _ _ _ _ _
13. VNSRAE _ _ _ _ _ _
15. NLNEO _ _ _ _ _
17. OMT _ _ _
18. NAAD _ _ _ _
19. KNSAH _ _ _ _ _
20. ICMIARCU _ _ _ _ _ _ _ _
24. RGNREA _ _ _ _ _ _
28. OBSKOR _ _ _ _ _ _
30. IABERD _ _ _ _ _ _
31. LLUMEN _ _ _ _ _ _
34. AGCIR _ _ _ _ _
35. VTESE _ _ _ _ _
38. AEETTSL _ _ _ _ _ _ _
39. EIORBB _ _ _ _ _ _
40. ENJOS _ _ _ _ _
43. OGLONSD _ _ _ _ _ _ _
44. UDLGO _ _ _ _ _
45. CERI _ _ _ _
47. EYLK _ _ _ _
48. RESTTAW _ _ _ _ _ _ _
51. ERSAK _ _ _ _ _
53. SIETERF _ _ _ _ _ _ _
55. AMTT _ _ _ _
56. ILBDNO _ _ _ _ _ _
58. MSTHI _ _ _ _ _
59. NGUYO _ _ _ _ _
61. KSPREAC _ _ _ _ _ _ _
64. ADYN _ _ _ _
65. AAICGR _ _ _ _ _ _
66. ELYLK _ _ _ _ _
67. RIEC _ _ _ _

DOWN

1. IPCANEKKRE _ _ _ _ _ _ _ _ _ _
2. LROYTA _ _ _ _ _ _
4. ANNOATM _ _ _ _ _ _ _
5. OTTL _ _ _ _
6. OERSNEPT _ _ _ _ _ _ _ _
8. AHNSHAAN _ _ _ _ _ _ _ _
9. RNOTNO _ _ _ _ _ _
14. MSOETRT _ _ _ _ _ _ _
16. LYARR _ _ _ _ _
21. LINOC _ _ _ _ _
22. NCIK _ _ _ _
23. BEFBILDUETSL _ _ _ _ _ _ _ _ _ _ _ _
25. LNALE _ _ _ _ _
26. BCRGA _ _ _ _ _
27. BRRAECTE _ _ _ _ _ _ _ _
29. ELE _ _ _
32. HGBRAUHA _ _ _ _ _ _ _ _
33. YALHE _ _ _ _ _
36. THESRA _ _ _ _ _ _
37. DOOLLAW _ _ _ _ _ _ _
39. SORREG _ _ _ _ _ _
41. ANWOMB _ _ _ _ _ _
42. NCKUBER _ _ _ _ _ _ _
46. AERTRC _ _ _ _ _ _
49. MIHST _ _ _ _ _
50. ATRTAY _ _ _ _ _ _
52. TANAALT _ _ _ _ _ _ _
54. NADWSO _ _ _ _ _ _
57. DYNEEN _ _ _ _ _ _
58. OPAUSL _ _ _ _ _ _
60. GREO _ _ _ _
62. RIDE _ _ _ _
63. ENK _ _ _

LXVII

MINNESOTA VIKINGS

ACROSS

1. Hall of Fame guard from Arizona State (1988-1999) who was a 1st round pick and an NFL record 12-time Pro Bowler. He is a member of the NFL 1990s All-Decade Team and is among "The 50 Greatest Vikings". He started 188 out of a possible 192 games for Minnesota, including every game in his last 10 seasons. He wore #64.

3. Hall of Fame receiver from Ohio State (1990-2001) who had been a 4th round pick by the Eagles (1987-1989). With the Vikings he was a Pro Bowler in 8 straight seasons, reaching 1,000 receiving yards in each of those years. He was also a 3-time NFL leader in touchdown catches. Minnesota has retired his #80.

5. The first name of the player referred to in 1 DOWN.

9. Defensive back from Ohio State (2004-2012) who had been a 1st round pick by the Bills (1999-2003). He was a 3-time Pro Bowler for Minnesota and is among "The 50 Greatest Vikings". His 21 interceptions are 10th most on the Viking all-time list. His son was a star defensive back for the Gophers. He wore #26.

11. Butkus Award-winning linebacker from UCLA (2015-2019) who was a 2nd round pick and has only played for the Vikings to date. He made his first Pro Bowl in 2019 and has started 70 out of a possible 80 regular season games. He wears #54.

12. The first name of the player referred to in 6 ACROSS.

13. 5'9", 185-pound running back from Stanford (1982-1989) who was a 2nd round pick by the Vikings. He is 7th on the all-time Viking rushing yards list and caught 250 passes but sadly, he may be best recalled for not catching that 4th quarter pass in the end zone at Washington in the NFC Championship Game in 1988. He wore #20.

16. Defensive back from Notre Dame (2012-2019) who was a 1st round pick and has only played for the Vikings to date. He is a 5-time Pro Bowler and his 23 career interceptions are the 7th most in team history. No Viking has ever had more than his 4 defensive touchdowns. He wears #22.

17. Gopher quarterback from Michigan (1973-1976) who went on to be a Super Bowl Champion as a Steeler defensive back (1979). He was the Viking defensive coordinator (1992-1995) and then, after a successful stint as the Tampa head coach, he went on to win a Super Bowl (2007) as head coach of the Colts (2002-2008).

18. Quarterback from East Texas State (1981-1991) who was an 8th round pick and a 1988 Pro Bowler. He went 27-21 as a starter and stands at #4 on the all-time Viking lists in passing yards and touchdown passes. He led the 1987 Wild Card team to the NFC Title Game, losing that heartbreaker in Washington. He wore #11.

19. Receiver from Grambling (1991-1999 & 2001) who was a 3rd round pick and had 4 straight years with 1,000+ receiving yards (1994-1997) for Minnesota. He made 12 plays of 50+ yards, the 2nd most in team history. He is #4 on the all-time Viking list in receiving yards, #5 in catches and #6 in scoring catches. He wore #86.

20. Colombian kicker from Tennessee (1990-1995) who came to the Vikings after playing for the Dolphins (1985-1988). He was a 1994 Pro Bowler who once made 31 straight field goal tries. His 133 successes are the 3rd most in Minnesota history. He wore #7.

22. Kicker from UCLA (2016-2017) who came to the Vikings after playing 4 years in Washington (2012-2015). His 47 field goals are 8th most in team history. His 53- yard field goal with 1:29 to play in that incredible play-off game in 2018 vs. the Saints came just before the "Minnesota Miracle". He wore #2.

27. Undrafted, Hall of Fame quarterback from Washington (1994-1996) who won 5 Grey Cups in the CFL before being a 6-time Pro Bowler with the Oilers (1984-1993). With Minnesota he was a 2-time Pro Bowler but went just 21-18 as a starter with no playoff wins. He was fared even worse with Seattle (1997-1998). He wore #1.

28. Linebacker from UCLA (2014-2019) who was a 1st round pick and taken 9th overall. He has only played for the Vikings and has made 4 Pro Bowls so far. He ended an OT game in Tampa in 2014 by forcing a fumble and returning it for a score. He will be always be hated in Green Bay for a play in October 2017. He wears #55.

29. Defensive end from USC (2010-2019) who was a 4th round pick and a 4-time Pro Bowler for the Vikings. His 74.5 sacks are 4th most in team history (a stat not kept in the days of Eiler and Page). In February 2020 he opted out of his contract and became a free agent in March. He wore #97.

31. Quarterback from Florida State (1992-1998 & 2005-2006) who was a 9th round pick by the Vikings. He went 28-18 as a starter for Minnesota and is 6th in team history in both passing yardage and scoring passes. He went on to be a 1999 Pro Bowler with Tampa and a 2003 Super Bowl Champion. He wore #14.

33. The first name of the player referred to in 22 DOWN.

34. Defensive back from Marshall (1983-1993) who was a 7th round pick and a 3- time Pro Bowler for the Vikings. He made 144 starts for Minnesota, including every game in 6 of his 11 seasons. His 29 career interceptions are the 6th most in team history. He has the same last name as a Viking back-up QB in the 70's. He wore #39.

35. Undrafted fullback and Duluth native from Augustana (2016-2019) who was a 2019 Pro Bowler. He has been a valuable lead blocker and a useful receiver out of the backfield. He goes by two initials but his first name is Cortez. He wears #30.

38. Running back/kick returner from Tulane (2004-2007) who was a 4th round pick by the Vikings. He made just 11 starts for Minnesota but had 4 games with 100+ rushing yards. He also caught 116 passes and had 2 punts returned for touchdowns. His average of 10.3 yards per return on 74 punts is a team record. He wore #30.

40. Offensive tackle from Ohio State (1995-2000) who was a 1st round pick and a Pro Bowler as a rookie. He only played for the Vikings and died of heat stroke in training camp prior to the 2001 season, a tragedy that brought changes in how NFL trainers/medical staffs deal with this problem. He wore #77.

41. The first name of the player referred to in 30 ACROSS.

42. Center from Pittsburgh (1993-1999) who was a 4th round pick-and a 2-time Pro Bowler for the Vikings. He started every game in 5 of his 7 seasons in Minnesota. He went on to become a Super Bowl Champion with the Bucs (2000-2002) by winning his very last game. He wore #62.

44. Receiver from Florida (2009-2012) who was a 1st round pick by the Vikings and the 2009 NFL Rookie of the Year. He had 280 catches for 3300 yards and was a constant scoring threat. He was also an electrifying kickoff returner, running back 5 for touchdowns. He later helped Seattle win a Super Bowl (2014). He wore #12.

45. South African kicker from Syracuse (1998-2002) who had earlier played for the Steelers and Eagles. His 109 field goals are the 5th most in Viking history. In 1998 he became the first kicker with a perfect regular season (35 for 35) but, of course, he missed that clinching field goal vs. Atlanta in the NFL Title Game. He wore #1.

50. The first name of the player referred to in 19 ACROSS.

52. Tight-end from Notre Dame (2011-2019) who was a 2nd round pick and has been a 2-time Pro Bowler. He has only played for Vikings to date. His 425 catches and 47 touchdown catches are both 5th most in team history. His game-ending OT catch in a playoff game in 2020 in New Orleans was a huge highlight. He wears #82.

53. Running back from Michigan (1996-1999) who had been a 2nd round pick by the Browns (1990-1995). He was the 1989 Rose Bowl MVP and a 1994 Pro Bowler. With the Vikings he made just 11 starts but still managed 1,689 rushing yards with 25 rushing touchdowns. He wore #44.

54. Receiver from Nevada (2003-2005) who was a 3rd round pick by the Vikings. He had 1,000 receiving yards for Minnesota in 2004 before moving on to Seattle (2006-2009) and Detroit (2010-2013). His older brother was a much-maligned for the Gopher basketball team (1999-2003). He wore #81.

55. Hall of Fame defensive end from Pittsburgh (1985-1993) who was a 1st round pick by the Vikings. He was a 5-time pro Bowler for Minnesota and led the NFL with 21 sacks in 1989. His 96.5 career sacks are the 2nd most in the recorded era and he is among "The 50 Greatest Vikings". He died of brain cancer in 2020. He wore #56.

57. Aptly-named linebacker from Illinois (1977-1990) who was a 9th round pick and only played for Minnesota, making 2 Pro Bowls. He played in 201 games for the Vikings and made 160 starts. He was the team's all-time leader in tackles when he retired and is among "The 50 Greatest Vikings". He wore #55.

61. Receiver from Western Michigan (2013-2014) who had been a 2nd round pick by the Packers (2006-2012), for whom he was a 2-time Pro Bowler. He had 3 straight years with 1,000+ receiving yards for Green Bay (2008-2010). With the Vikings he had 68 catches in 2013 and 59 in 2014. He wore #15.

64. The first name of the player referred to in 15 DOWN.

65. Kicker from Georgia (2012-2016) who was a 6th round pick by the Vikings and a Pro Bowler as a rookie. That year he tied the NFL rookie record with 35 field goals and went 10 for 10 from 50+ yards. His 133 field goals are the 4th most in team history but he is mainly known for that crushing playoff failure in 2016. He wore #3.

66. Receiver from Fresno State (2008-2011) who had been a 3rd round pick by the Bears (2004-2007), whom he helped to reach the 2007 Super Bowl. He had a career best 964 receiving yards with the Vikings in 2008. That season he jolted the Bears with a 99-yard touchdown connection. He wore #87.

67. The first name of the player referred to in 28 ACROSS.

68. The first name of the player referred to in 30 DOWN.

DOWN

1. Defensive tackle from Washington State (1985-1991) who was a 1st round pick by the Vikings and a 2-time Pro Bowler. He was the 1989 NFL Defensive Player of the Year when he had 18 sacks. He is a member of the NFL 1980s All-Decade Team and is among "The 50 Greatest Vikings". He wore #75.

2. Defensive end from Idaho State (2008-2013) who had been a 4th round pick by the Chiefs (2004-2007). With the Vikings he was a 4-time Pro Bowler, the NFC Defensive Player of the Year (2011) and the NFL sack leader (2011) with a team record of 22. He is among "The 50 Greatest Vikings". He wore #69.

3. Running back from Florida State (2017-2019) who was a 2nd round pick by the Vikings and a 2019 Pro Bowler. His first 2 seasons were injury-marred but in 2019 he had 1,135 rushing yards with 13 touchdowns plus 53 catches. He wears #33.

4. Undrafted receiver from Minnesota State (2013-2019) who has made 2 Pro Bowls to date (2017 & 2018). He went from being a special teamer to a star, with 69 catches in his break-out year of 2016, 91 catches for 1,276 yards in 2017 and then 113 catches for 1,373 yards in 2018. He was hurt for much of 2019. He wears #19.

MINNESOTA VIKINGS

6. Hall of Fame guard from Michigan (2006-2011) who had been a 1st round pick by Seattle (2001-2005). He was a 4-time Pro Bowler with the Vikings and started every game from 2006 through 2009. He wore #76.

7. Receiver from South Carolina (2007-2012) who was a 2nd round pick by the Vikings and a 2009 Pro Bowler. Often injured, he had one superb season with 1,300 receiving yards in 2009, followed by a 3-touchdown performance in a post-season demolition of Dallas. He ended with 3 semi-productive years in Seattle. He wore #18.

8. Quarterback from Rice (1977-1989) who was a 1st round pick by Minnesota and a 1986 Pro Bowler. He was the first NFL player to twice pass for 450 yards in a game. He is among the "50 Greatest Vikings" and he is #2 in team history in completions, passing yardage and touchdown passes, behind only Fran Tarkenton. He wore #9.

10. Viking head coach (1992-2001) whose Viking record, including the post-season, was 101-70. Only Bud Grant won more games for Minnesota. He had earlier been the head coach at Northwestern (1981-1985) and Stanford (1989-1991) and he finished with an unhappy tenure as Arizona Cardinal head coach (2004-2006).

14. Running back from Ohio State (1993-2000) who was a 1st round pick and only played for the Vikings. He was a graceful, long-striding sprinter who ran for 1,000+ yards in each of his last 4 seasons. His 6,818 career rushing yards are the 2nd most in team history. He wore #26.

15. Randall Cunningham played college football at
_____.

20. Undrafted, Hall of Fame defensive tackle from Texas A&M-Kingsville (1990-2000) who was a 6-time Pro Bowler for the Vikings and the 1997 NFL sacks leader. His 114 career sacks are the most in team history. He is a member of the Vikings Ring of Honor and he started every game for 8 straight seasons (1993-2000). He wore #93.

21. The first name of the player referred to in 16 ACROSS.

23. St. Paul native and Harvard grad who was Minnesota's center (1998-2008). He was a 6th round pick and a 6-time Pro Bowler for the Vikings. He was also a 6-time Viking Man of the Year in recognition of his tireless charity work. He started every game in 7 of his 11 seasons with Minnesota. He wore #75 & #78.

24. Hall of Fame receiver from Marshall (1998-2004 & 2010) who was a 1st round pick, a 5-time Pro Bowler and a 3-time NFL leader in touchdown catches while with Minnesota. He is 2nd all-time for the Vikings in catches, receiving yardage and catches. He finally made it to a Super Bowl with the 2007 Patriots. He wore #84.

25. The first name used by a running back from Kentucky (1996-2000 & 2002-2005) who was a 3rd round pick by the Vikings. He had 1,500 career rushing yards and caught 130 passes for the Vikings but he is best recalled as the recipient of a brilliant, no-look lateral on the final play of a half by 16 DOWN. He wore #21 & #20.

26. Defensive back from Southwestern Louisiana (1995-2001) who was a 2nd round pick and only played for the Vikings. He was a 1995 Pro Bowler when he led the NFL with 9 interceptions. His 22 career interceptions are the 8th most in team history. He died at age 42 from ALS complications. He wore #42.

28. Running back from Wisconsin (2001-20 05) who was a 1st round pick by the Vikings. He was 2002 Pro Bowler when had his only 1,000-yard rushing season. His 3,174 career rushing yards are the 9th most in team history. In 2017 he was given a 5-year sentence for burglary and identity theft. He wore #23.

30. Quarterback from Tulsa (2003-2004 & 2008) who was mainly a back-up but did post a 10-3 record as a starter for Minnesota. He first played 5 years in Washington (1994-1998), for whom he gained some unwanted notoriety for his ill-advised celebratory head-butt of an unpadded wall in the Meadowlands. He wore #12.

32. Linebacker from Iowa (2006-2016) who was a 1st round pick and a 2-time Pro Bowler. He only played for the Vikings and he led the NFC in tackles in 2010. He made 144 career starts, including every game in 6 of his 11 seasons. In 2015 he returned an interception 91 yards for a touchdown vs. the Chargers. He wore #52.

33. Quarterback from Delaware (1987-1992) who was a 4th round pick by Minnesota. He went 19-16 as a starter for the Vikings but with the Raiders (1999-2004) he was a 4-time Pro Bowler. In 2002 he was the NFL Most Valuable Player, the season he led Oakland to a humiliating loss in the Super Bowl. He wore #16.

35. Defensive end and Jamaica native from LSU (2015-2019) who was a 3rd round pick by the Vikings and has made 2 Pro Bowls to date. He is the youngest player in NFL history to reach 50 career sacks and he has started every game in the past 3 seasons (2017-2019). He wears #99.

36. The first name of the player referred to in 14 DOWN.

37. Viking head coach (1986-1991) who went 55-46 in the regular season and led Minnesota to the 1987 NFC Championship Game as a Wild Card team. He had earlier been the Viking offensive coordinator (1968-1985), during which time Minnesota won 11 division titles and appeared in 4 Super Bowls.

39. Defensive back from USC (1983-1991) who was a 1st round pick and a 6-time Pro Bowler for the Vikings. He is a member of the NFL 1980s All-Decade Team and the Viking Ring of Honor and he is among "The 50 Greatest Vikings" as well. His 37 career interceptions are the 4th most in team history. He wore #47.

42. Slightly-built but electric, receiver from Michigan (1985-1993) who-came to the Vikings after playing 3 years in the USFL. He was a 3-time Pro Bowler with Minnesota and is among "The 50 Greatest Vikings". He had 3 years with 1,000+ receiving yards and his 478 career catches are the 4th most in team history. He wore #81.

43. Defensive tackle from Oklahoma State (2003-2013) who was a 1st round pick by the Vikings and taken 9th overall. He was a 6-time Pro Bowler for Minnesota and is a member of the NFL 2000s All-Decade Team. He is also among "The 50 Greatest Vikings". Besides being a force in the middle, he also had 60 sacks. He wore #93.

46. Offensive lineman from Cal (1994-2000) who was a 1st round pick and a 2-time Pro Bowler for Minnesota. He helped the 1998 and 2000 teams reach NFC Championship Games and finally reached the Super Bowl with the 2003 Panthers. He finished up with the Bucs (2004-2005) and Rams (2006-2007). He wore #73.

47. The first name of the player referred to in 11 ACROSS.

48. Defensive tackle and Virgin Islands native (2014-2019) who had been a 2nd round pick by the Giants, for whom he was a 2012 Super Bowl Champion. He was a 2-time Pro Bowler for Minnesota and was a superb run-stopper. In 2018 he lumbered 65 yards to score a crucial touchdown in a win at Philadelphia. He wore #98.

49. The first name of the player referred to in 11 DOWN.

51. Undrafted kicker from Cal (2006-2011) who began with the Packers (1997-2005), earning membership in the Green Bay Hall of Fame. He made 86% of his field goal tries for the Vikings and his 135 successes are the 2nd most in Viking history. No player in NFL history scored more points without making a Pro Bowl. He wore #8.

55. Linebacker from USC (1992-1995) who had earlier played 7 seasons with the Saints, Chiefs and Cowboys (1985-1991). He made his only Pro Bowl with the Vikings (1994). He went on to be the head coach of the Panthers (2003-2011) and Raiders (2015-2017). He wore #55.

56. The first name of the player referred to in 4 DOWN.

58. The first name of the player referred to in 26 DOWN.

59. Offensive tackle from USC (2012-2016) who was a 1st round pick and taken 4th overall by the Vikings. He was a Pro Bowler as a rookie then missed nearly all of 2016 due to injury. The Vikings let him move on to Carolina (2017-2018). He has to be seen as a disappointment in view of his college fame and high draft status. He wore #75.

60. 6'7" Viking head coach (2002-2005) who had been an NFL tight end (1992-1995). The Vikings went just 33-34 in his tenure and 1-1 in the post-season. The Minnetonka Boat Scandal is thought by many to have been instrumental in his firing. Since then he has been an assistant coach with the Jaguars, Bears, Falcons and Raiders.

61. The first name of the player referred to in 19 DOWN.

62. The first name of the coach referred to in 7 ACROSS.

63. The first name of the player referred to in 23 DOWN.

MINNESOTA VIKINGS

MINNESOTA VIKINGS

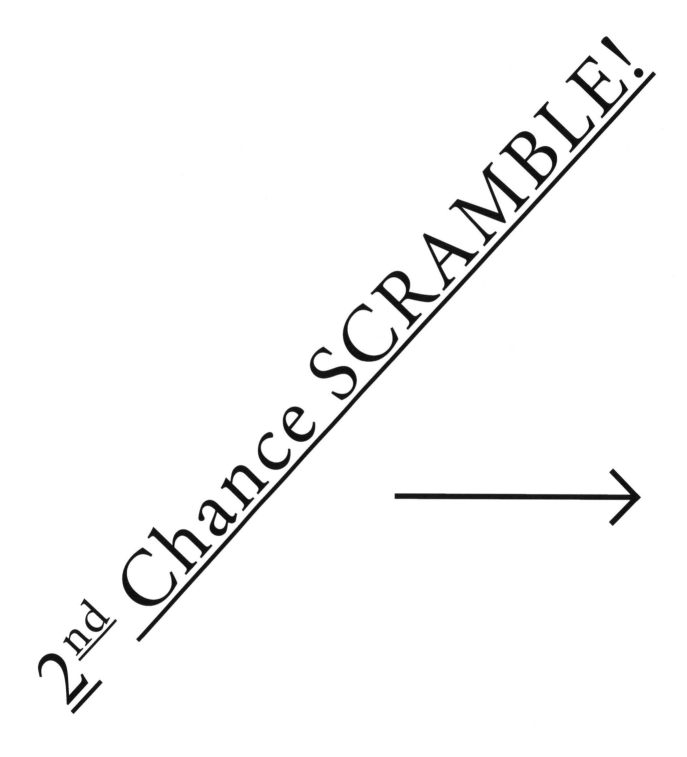

MINNESOTA VIKINGS

ACROSS

1. AEMLNIDC ＿＿＿＿＿＿＿＿
3. RACTER ＿＿＿＿＿＿
5. EHKTI ＿＿＿＿＿
9. NIFDILEW ＿＿＿＿＿＿＿＿
11. CEDKSNKIR ＿＿＿＿＿＿＿＿＿
12. RCIE ＿＿＿＿
13. NENOSL ＿＿＿＿＿＿
16. TSMIH ＿＿＿＿＿
17. DNYGU ＿＿＿＿＿
18. LISWNO ＿＿＿＿＿＿
19. DRE ＿＿＿
20. EIREZV ＿＿＿＿＿＿
22. OFHTRA ＿＿＿＿＿＿
27. NOOM ＿＿＿＿
28. ARBR ＿＿＿＿
29. RFINEFG ＿＿＿＿＿＿＿
31. SOONHJN ＿＿＿＿＿＿＿
33. USG ＿＿＿
34. LEE ＿＿＿
35. HAM ＿＿＿
38. OROEM ＿＿＿＿＿
40. GINTERSR ＿＿＿＿＿＿＿＿
41. NAET ＿＿＿＿
42. RSTIYCH ＿＿＿＿＿＿＿
44. HANIVR ＿＿＿＿＿＿
45. ARENDNSO ＿＿＿＿＿＿＿＿
50. ALCR ＿＿＿＿
52. URHODPL ＿＿＿＿＿＿＿
53. HRAOD ＿＿＿＿＿
54. UEOSLRNB ＿＿＿＿＿＿＿＿
55. DNLMOEA ＿＿＿＿＿＿＿
57. ULLTDSEW ＿＿＿＿＿＿＿＿
61. NSINNGJE ＿＿＿＿＿＿＿＿
64. ANLOROD ＿＿＿＿＿＿＿
65. SLWAH ＿＿＿＿＿
66. BEANRIR ＿＿＿＿＿＿＿
67. YKEL ＿＿＿＿
68. DDTO ＿＿＿＿

DOWN

1. DALLRIM ＿＿＿＿＿＿＿
2. EALNL ＿＿＿＿＿
3. OCKO ＿＿＿＿
4. ELNEHIT ＿＿＿＿＿＿＿
6. TSCINHHUNO ＿＿＿＿＿＿＿＿＿＿
7. IRCE ＿＿＿＿
8. KAREMR ＿＿＿＿＿＿
10. ERGNE ＿＿＿＿＿
14. TISHM ＿＿＿＿＿
15. NULV ＿＿＿＿
20. RDAENL ＿＿＿＿＿＿
21. NOESERV ＿＿＿＿＿＿＿
23. KRIB ＿＿＿＿
24. OSSM ＿＿＿＿
25. OEM ＿＿＿
26. AOHSMT ＿＿＿＿＿＿
28. BTTEENN ＿＿＿＿＿＿＿
30. TREFEORT ＿＿＿＿＿＿＿＿
32. NGAEYWER ＿＿＿＿＿＿＿＿
33. NNAOGN ＿＿＿＿＿＿
35. RNEHTU ＿＿＿＿＿＿
36. MATT ＿＿＿＿
37. SRUNB ＿＿＿＿＿
39. OENRBRW ＿＿＿＿＿＿＿
42. ARTECR ＿＿＿＿＿＿
43. LSWLMIIA ＿＿＿＿＿＿＿＿
46. SESUTEIS ＿＿＿＿＿＿＿＿
47. FAUD ＿＿＿＿
48. PEJOSH ＿＿＿＿＿＿
49. ONHJ ＿＿＿＿
51. GLELOWLN ＿＿＿＿＿＿＿＿
55. RLIEDO ＿＿＿＿＿＿
56. AMAD ＿＿＿＿
58. NILAVL ＿＿＿＿＿＿
59. LLIKA ＿＿＿＿＿
60. ETCI ＿＿＿＿
61. JOEY ＿＿＿＿
62. YOTN ＿＿＿＿
63. CHDA ＿＿＿＿

TAMPA BUCCANEERS

ACROSS

1. Heisman-winning quarterback from Miami (1987-1992) who was taken 1st overall by Tampa. He went just 24-48 as a starter for the Bucs with 112 interceptions against just 77 touchdown passes. He went on to play 15 more seasons with the Browns, Ravens, Jets Cowboys and Panthers. He wore #14.

6. Receiver from Ohio State (2004-2008) who had been a 1st round pick by Seattle (1995-1999). He came to the Bucs after a stop in Dallas (2000-2003) and had 3 straight years with 1,000+ receiving yards for Tampa. He is the only player in NFL history with 10,000 receiving yards and no Pro Bowl appearances. He wore #84.

9. Quarterback from Florida State (2015-2019) who was taken 1st overall by Tampa. He was a 2015 Pro Bowler and he led the NFL in both passing yards and interceptions in 2019. He went 28-42 as a starter for the Bucs and is #1 all-time for the team in both passing yards and touchdown passes. He wore #3.

11. Defensive back from Virginia (1997-2012) who was a 3rd round pick and only played for the Bucs. He was a 5-time Pro Bowler and a 2003 Super Bowl Champion. He is #1 all-time for Tampa with 47 career interceptions and is a member of the team's Honor Roll. He started every game in 13 straight seasons! He wore #20.

12. Tampa head coach (2019) who went 7-9 in his first season. He had earlier been the head man in Arizona (2013-2017), where his teams went 49-30-1 and made the playoffs twice.

13. Linebacker from Nebraska (2012-2019) who was a 2nd round pick and has only played for the Bucs to date. He was a 2015 Pro Bowler and has made 121 starts for Tampa, averaging 15 starts per season. He is #3 all-time for the franchise with 724 solo tackles #1 with 14 fumble recoveries. He wears #54.

14. So far, the Bucs have made the playoffs in _____ different seasons.

17. Quarterback from Florida State (2001-2004) who had been a 9th round pick by Minnesota (1992-1998), for whom he went 28-18 as a starter. Before coming to the Bucs he was a 1999 Pro Bowler with Washington. He was a 2002 Pro Bowler for the Tampa team that went on to win the 2003 Super Bowl. He wore #14.

18. Running back from Tennessee (1990-1993) who was a 2nd round pick by the Bucs, for whom he had a career-best 1,171 rushing yards in 1992. He had 500 rushing yards for the 1994 Packers but never averaged 4 yards per carry in any of his 7 NFL seasons. He died of a heart attack at age 50 in 2019. He wore #33 & #34.

20. The first name of the player referred to in 31 DOWN.

25. Quarterback from Fresno State (1994-1999) who was taken 6th overall by the Bucs, for whom he was a 1999 Pro Bowler. He went 38-38 as a starter for Tampa and had 80 interceptions against just 70 touchdown passes. Backed by a fierce defense, he became a Super Bowl Champion with the 2000 Ravens. He wore #12.

26. Running back from Fresno State (2002-2007) who had been a 4th round pick by Arizona (1998-2001). With the Bucs, he had 700 rushing yards in the 2002 regular season and 124 rushing yards in the ensuing Super Bowl. He had a career-best 900 rushing yards in 2004 and is #7 for the team in career rushing yards. He wore #32.

29. Quarterback from Tularie (1999-2003) who was a 2nd round pick by the Bucs. He went 14-8 as a starter for Tampa, 10-6 in his best season (2000), in which he passed for 2,700 yards. For the 2002 team that won the Super Bowl, he threw just 27 passes. He was out of the NFL at age 27. He wore #10.

31. In the 2003 Super Bowl, the Bucs rolled over the _____ by a score of 48-21.

34. The first name of the player referred to in 14 ACROSS.

35. The first name of the player referred to in 32 ACROSS.

TAMPA BUCCANEERS

38. The first name of the player referred to in 27 ACROSS.

39. Receiver from USC (2000-2003) who had been taken 1st overall by the Jets (1996-1999), for whom he had 2 years with 1,000+ receiving yards. He was a 2001 Pro Bowler for the Bucs when he had 1,200 receiving yards and he had 1,000 for the team that won the 2003 Super Bowl. He wore #19.

41. The first name of the coach referred to in 6 ACROSS.

44. Guard from Oklahoma (2006-2013) who was a 1st round pick and 2-time Pro Bowler for the Bucs. He made 112 starts for Tampa, averaging 15 starts per season. He missed all of 2012 due to injury but bounced back to start very game in 2013. He finished by making 13 starts for the 2014 Rams. He wore #75.

46. Kicker from Argentina and Kansas State (1999-2003) who was a 3rd round pick by the Bucs. He was a 2000 Pro Bowler and 2003 Super Bowl Champion for Tampa, with 2 field goals in that 48-21 romp. His 137 career field goals are the most in franchise history. He wore #7.

47. _____ was the dominant color of the Buccaneer uniforms from 1976 through 1996.

48. The first name of the player referred to in 3 ACROSS.

49. Quarterback from Michigan (2004-2005) who had been a 3rd round pick by Denver (1998-2002), for whom he made his only Pro Bowl in 2000. He spent 2003 with Miami before coming to Tampa, for whom he went 12-9 as a starter. He is the son of a an NFL Hall of Fame quarterback. He wore #14.

53. From 1976-1996, the face of a swashbuckling pirate adorned the sides of the team's helmets. He was referred to as "_____ Bruce."

55. The Buccaneers have been beaten 39 times to date by the _____; the most losses suffered at the hands of any opponent.

56. The Buccaneers have beaten the _____ 27 times to date, making them Tampa's favorite opponent.

58. Quarterback from San Jose state (2007-2008) who had been a 1996 CFL Grey Cup Champion before coming to the NFL. He played for the 49ers, Browns, Lions and Eagles before arriving in Tampa, for whom he made the last of his 4 Pro Bowls in 2007. He went 14-10 as a starter for the Bucs and wore #7.

61. Cornerback from Auburn (2019-2021) who was a 3rd round pick by the Bucs. He went on the Covid list in Week 15 in 2021 and has played in 40 games for Tampa to date. He has made 23 starts and recorded 5 interceptions, with one returned for a touchdown in 2020. He wears #35.

62. Defensive end from Illinois (2001-2006) who had been taken 3rd overall by Arizona (1996-2000). With the Bucs, he was a 2-time Pro Bowler and a 2003 Super Bowl Champion. His 69.5 career sacks are #2 all-time for the Bucs. (The NFL has only recognized this stat since 1982). He wore #97.

64. Running back from Florida (1994-1997) who was a 2nd round pick by the Bucs. He had 1,000+ rushing yards in both of his first 2 seasons but never again approached those numbers with Tampa. He did, however, run for 850 yards for the 1999 Ravens. He wore #32.

66. The first name of the Tampa head coach (1996-2001) who ended a streak of 14 losing seasons for the team and was its first coach to post consecutive winning seasons. His teams went 54-42 and it was HIS players who won the 2003 Super Bowl. He later won his own Super Bowl with the 2006 Colts.

67. Defensive back from USC (1998-2007) who was a 2nd round pick by the Bucs and a Super Bowl Champion with the 2002 team, for whom he led the NFL with 8 interceptions. He made 89 starts for Tampa and his 22 career interceptions are #7 all-time for the franchise. He wore #25.

70. The pants that the Bucs have worn since 1997 are a shade of grey that is called _____.

71. Quarterback from Kansas State (2009-2013) who was a 1st round pick by the Bucs and went 25-36 as a starter. His best season was 2010 when led the team to a 10-6 record. In 2013 he was released after a 0-3 start. His 80 career touchdown passes are #2 all-time for the Bucs. He wore #5.

72. Running back from Boise State (2012-2017) who was a 1st round pick and 2-time Pro Bowler for the Bucs. He had 2 years with 1,400+ rushing yards for Tampa (2012 & 2015) but 2016 & 2017 were disappointing due to a substance abuse suspension and a groin injury. He had 4,600 rushing yards for Tampa and wore #22.

DOWN

2. Quarterback from Miami (1992-1994) who was a 5th round pick by the Bucs and had been a 2-time NCAA Champion with Miami. He went just 11-18 as a starter for Tampa but did manage to pass for 2,900 yards and 16 touchdowns in 1994. He is #8 all-time for Tampa with 34 scoring passes. He wore #7.

3. Wandering, journeyman quarterback from San Jose State (1984-1987 & 1992-1993) who had been a 10th round pick by the 49ers (1977-1980). He came to Tampa from Denver (1981-1983) and also played for the Chiefs, Dolphins and Falcons in his 21-year career. He went 8-29 as a starter for Tampa and wore #17.

4. 6'5", 230-pound receiver from Northern Colorado (2012-2016) who had been a 2nd round pick by the Chargers (2005-2011), for whom he was a 2-time Pro Bowler. He had 3 years with 1,000+ receiving yards for San Diego and then 3 more for Tampa. His 4,300 receiving yards are #4 for all-time for the Bucs. He wore #83.

5. Receiver from Pitt (2008-2009) who had been a 2nd round pick by Dallas (2002-2004). He had 1,000 receiving yards for the 2005 Browns but missed all of 2007 with a substance abuse problem. He went on to Tampa and was the NFL Comeback Player of the Year with 1,200 receiving yards in 2008. He wore #81.

7. Defensive back from East Tennessee (1996-2001) who was a 3rd round pick by the Bucs and the NFL leader in interceptions with 7 in 1999. He was a 2000 Pro Bowler for Tampa and then finished with the Jets (2002-2004). He is #2 all-time for the Bucs with 31 career interceptions. He wore #21.

8. The first name of the player referred to in 9 ACROSS.

10. Tampa head coach (2014:-2015) whose teams went 2-14 and 6-10. He had earlier been the Chicago head coach (2004-2012) and taken the Bears to the 2007 Super Bowl. He is currently trying to revive the program at Illinois.

15. Linebacker from Cal (1993-1999) who had been a 5th round pick by Pittsburgh (1987-1992). He was a 5-time Pro Bowler for the Bucs and is a member of the NFL 1990s All-Decade Team. He made 104 starts for Tampa, including every game in 5 of his 7 seasons. His 681 solo tackles are #4 for all-time for the Bucs. He wore #56.

16. Receiver from Penn State (2017-2019) who was a 3rd round pick by the Bucs and a 2019 Pro Bowler when he broke out with 86 catches for 1,300 yards. He wears #14.

19. Linebacker from Florida State (1995-2008) who was a 1st round pick by Tampa and only played for the Bucs. He was an 11-time Pro Bowler and a Super Bowl Champion with the 2002 team, for whom he was the NFL Defensive Player of the Year. He started every game in each of his first 13 seasons and his #55 has been retired.

21. On the way to the Super Bowl, the 2002 Buccaneers beat the _____ in the NFC Championship Game by a score of 27-10.

22. The first name of the player referred to in 18 ACROSS.

23. Workhorse running back from Missouri (1981-1989) who was a 2nd round pick and 1984 Pro

Bowler for the Bucs, for whom he had 2 years with 1,300+ rushing yards. His 5,900 career rushing yards are #1 all-time for Tampa. In addition, he is #2 all-time with 430 catches. He wore #32.

24. To date, the Buccaneers have won _____ division titles.

27. The first name of the player referred to in 35 DOWN.

28. Buccaneer head coach (2016-2018) whose teams went 9-7, 5-11 and 5-11. He had earlier been the offensive coordinator for Atlanta (2012-2014) and Tampa (2015). In 2019 he resumed his duties as offensive coordinator for the Falcons.

30. The first name of the coach referred to in 22 DOWN.

31. Defensive back from San Diego's Torrey Pines High and Stanford (1993-2003), who was a 3rd round pick by the Bucs, a 5-time Pro Bowler and a 2003 Super Bowl Champion. He went on to make 4 more Pro Bowls with Denver (2004-2007) and he is a member of the Ring of Honor for both franchises. He is now the 49er's GM. He wore #47.

33. Running back from Auburn (2005-2010) who was taken 5th overall by the Bucs, for whom he was the NFL Offensive Rookie of the Year when he had 1,178 rushing yards. Injuries prevented him from coming close to those numbers again however. His real name is Carnell but he goes by a flashy nickname. He wore #24.

35 5'9", 185-pound running back from Florida State (1997-2001 and 2008) who was a 1st round pick by the Bucs and a 2-time Pro Bowler. He had 2 years with 1,000+ rushing yards for Tampa and then 3 more with Atlanta (2002-2007). His 4,900 career rushing yards are #3 all-time for the Bucs. He wore #28.

36. Undrafted kicker from Baylor (2005-2008) who had come to the NFL with the Giants (2002-2003). His 98 field goals are #4 all-time for the Bucs. He

then went on to kick 259 field goals for Atlanta, making the 2016 Pro Bowl and kicking 34 field goals for the NFC Champions that melted down in the Super Bowl. He wore #3.

37. Defensive tackle from Oklahoma (2010-2018) who was taken 3rd overall by the Bucs and was a 6-time Pro Bowler. He made 123 starts for Tampa and was a superb run stopper with enough agility to record 54.5 sacks, the 3rd most in franchise history. He spent 2019 with Carolina and will be with Dallas in 2020. He wore #93.

40. Hall of Fame defensive tackle from Miami (1995-2003) who was a 1st round pick, a 7-time Pro Bowler and a 2003 Super Bowl Champ for Tampa. He was the 1999 NFL Defensive Player of the Year and is a member of the NFL 1990s All-Decade Team. His #99 has been retired but he has not been a good citizen in retirement.

42. Since 1998, the Buccaneers have played their home game in Raymond _____ Stadium.

43. The first name of the player referred to in 16 ACROSS.

45. Tampa head coach (2012-2013) whose teams went 7-9 and 4-12. He had earlier been a success as the head coach at Rutgers (2001-2011) and he has gone back to Rutgers for 2020.

48. Defensive back from Pitt (2013) who had been a 1st round pick and a 4-time Pro Bowler for the Jets (2007-2012). He also made the Pro Bowl in his only year with the Bucs. He helped the 2014 Patriots win the Super Bowl before going back to the Jets (2015-2016). He wore #24.

50. The first name of the player referred to in 16 DOWN.

51. Tampa head coach (2002-2008) who led his first team to a Super Bowl Championship. He had earlier been the head coach of the Raiders (1998-2001) and he went back to Oakland in 2018 after being given an obscene amount of cash to come out of retirement.

52. 250-pound running back from Purdue (1996-2007) who was a 2nd round pick, a 6-time Pro Bowler and a 2003 Super Bowl Champion for the Bucs. He only played for Tampa and is a member of the team's Ring of Honor. He is #1 all-time for the Bucs with 58 rushing touchdowns and #2 with 5,088 rushing yards. He wore #40.

54. Receiver from LSU (2004-2009) who was a 1st round pick by Tampa. He had a career-best 1,193 receiving yards as a rookie but never had another year like that due to injuries and just plain poor play. He wore #80.

57. Undrafted kicker from North Carolina (2009-2013 & 2015) who came to the NFL with the Chiefs (2008). His 114 field goals are #3 all-time for the Bucs and his 84% success rate is #1. He went on to kick for the Bears (2016-2017). He wore #5.

59. Receiver from Nicholls State (1987-1992) who was a 3rd round pick by the Bucs. He had a career-year with 1,400 receiving yards in 1989 and went on to have 1,000 receiving yards for the 1995 Panthers. His 5,018 career receiving yards are #2 alltime for the Bucs. He wore #89 & #88.

60. Receiver from Syracuse (2010-2013) who was a 4th round pick by the Bucs. He had 60+ catches in each of his first 3 seasons and 900+ receiving yards in both 2010 and 2012. He was hurt for most of 2013 and out of the NFL at age 27. He wore #19.

63. Buccaneer head coach (1992-1995) whose teams went just 23-41 with no winning seasons. He had earlier been the head man in Cincinnati (1984-1991) and his 1988 team was ahead in the final minute of the Super Bowl before Joe Montana secured a 20-16 win with a final dramatic touchdown pass to John Taylor.

65. Undrafted kicker from Virginia (1993-1998). His 117 field goals are #2 all-time for the Bucs but he had just a 73% success rate. He finished up with the 1999 Raiders. He wore #5.

68. 6'5", 230-pound receiver from Texas A&M (2014-2019) who was taken 7th overall by the Bucs and has made 3 Pro Bowls to date. He has only played for Tampa and has recorded 1,000+ receiving yards and 68+ catches in each of his 6 seasons with the team. He made Johnny Manziel's 2013 Heisman happen. He wears #13.

69. The first name of the player referred to in 9 DOWN.

TAMPA BUCCANEERS

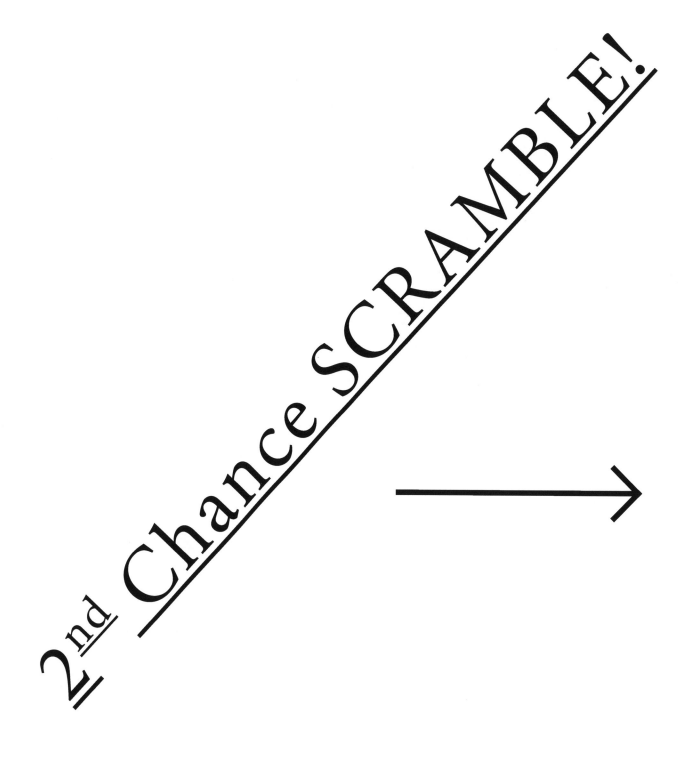

TAMPA BUCCANEERS

ACROSS

1. DTERAETEVS _____
6. LAOLGWYA _____
9. IWTNOSN _____
11. RBBERA _____
12. IARASN _____
13. ADIVD _____
14. NTE _____
17. JSOHONN _____
18. BOCB _____
20. IKME _____
25. DEIRFL _____
26. NMATTPI _____
29. INKG _____
31. AESRRID _____
34. ENTRT _____
35. DGOU _____
38. FJEF _____
39. OJNHOSN _____
41. RUCBE _____
44. PEJHSO _____
46. GRMAIACTA _____
47. OARNEG _____
48. ODENR _____
49. EIRESG _____
53. OCBUC _____
55. ESARB _____
56. ILNOS _____
58. GRACIA _____
61. ADNE _____
62. IECR _____
64. ERTTH _____
66. TYNO _____
67. LKEYL _____
70. WETEPR _____
71. RNEMFEA _____
72. TRMIAN _____

DOWN

2. IERCSOKN _____
3. RDEEBG _____
4. NJKSCAO _____
5. ABNTYR _____
7. ABAMAHR _____
8. BRDA _____
10. STMIH _____
15. RKNCOEINS _____
16. OIWNGD _____
19. KSROOB _____
21. EGSLAE _____
22. RNTIMA _____
23. WLEDIR _____
24. XSI _____
27. IEKM _____
28. TROETKE _____
30. GERG _____
31. YHNCL _____
33. ALWIILMS _____
35. NDNU _____
36. BYNRTA _____
37. YCMOC _____
40. APSP _____
42. SMJEA _____
43. HWAYSNEK _____
45. ISCOANH _____
48. IRSEV _____
50. NOJH _____
51. NDURGE _____
52. LSTOATT _____
54. YLOCNAT _____
57. TBHRA _____
59. ERIRRCA _____
60. LIIWMLAS _____
63. HYCEW _____
65. DSEHUT _____
68. NESVA _____
69. RSIHC _____

SEATTLE SEAHAWKS

ACROSS

1. Outspoken defensive back from Stanford (2011-2017) who was a 5th round pick by Seattle, a 4-time Pro Bowler and the 2013 NFL interceptions leader. He played in two Super Bowls for the Hawks winning in 2014. His 32 picks are #4 in franchise history. He went on the 49ers (2018-2020) and then Tampa (2021). He wore #25.

5. Defensive back from Washington State (2003-2012) who was a 1st round pick and only played for Seattle. He was a 2007 Pro Bowler and he is a member of the Seahawk 35th Anniversary team. He started every game in 5 different seasons and he is #7 alltime for Seattle with 21 interceptions and his #6 in solo tackles. He wore #23.

10. Receiver from North Carolina State (2001-2005 and 2008) who was a 1st round pick by Seattle. He is #9 all-time for the Seahawks in both catches (244) and receiving yardage (3,567). Between his two stints with Seattle, he was a 2005 Pro Bowler as a kick returner with Minnesota. He wore #81.

11. Linebacker from Michigan State (2006-2008) who had been a 1st round pick by the 49ers (2000-2005). He was a 5-time Pro Bowler, twice with Seattle. He started every game in each of his 3 seasons as a Seahawk and then finished up with 28 starts for the Lions (2009-2010). He wore #59 and #98.

13. The first name of the player referred to in 10 ACROSS.

14. The first name of the player referred to in 4 DOWN.

15. Running back from Oklahoma State (2017-2021) who, despite being just a 7th round pick by Seattle, had two seasons with 1,100 rushing yards. Injuries ruined his 2020 and 2021 seasons but he is still #8 all-time for the Seahawks with 3,502 rushing yards and #6 with 24 rushing touchdowns. He wears #32.

16. Center from Oregon (2009-2014) who was a 2nd round pick by Seattle and a 2-time Pro Bowler. He made 67 starts for the Seahawks and played in two Super Bowls, winning in 2014. With the Saints (2015-2018) he made another 63 starts and was a 2018 Pro Bowler. He wore #60.

19. 5'10", possession-type receiver from Penn State (2002-2008) who had been a 2nd round pick by the Bears (1996-2000). He is #6 all-time for Seattle with 4,869 receiving yards and #7 with 399 catches. His 94 catches in 2007 are tied for the 2nd most in team history. He wore #84.

20. Samoan-American linebacker from USC (2005-2010) who was a 2nd round pick and only played for Seattle. He was a 3-time Pro Bowler and helped the Seahawks reach the 2006 Super Bowl. He started every game in 4 of his 6 seasons. His dad was also from USC and was a fierce running back for the Patriots (1978-1990). He wore #51.

21. Running back from Penn State (1983-1989) who was taken 3rd overall by Seattle. He was a 3-time Pro Bowler for the Seahawks and a 2-time AFC Offensive Player of the Year. He had 3 years with 1,000+ rushing yards for Seattle and his 6,705 rushing yards are #3 all-time for the Seahawks. He wore #28.

23. Linebacker from Mississippi State (2011-2020) who was a 4th round pick by Seattle and played two Super Bowls, winning in 2014. He was a 2016 Pro Bowler and made 140 starts for the Seahawks. He is #4 all-time for Seattle with 593 solo tackles. In 2021 he moved on the Raiders. He wore #50.

25. Undrafted quarterback from Central Washington (1996-2000) who went 18-15 for Seattle as a starter. He went on to play for the Bengals, Lions and Cowboys (2001-2011) and had a composite record of 32-59 for those teams. His 49 touchdown passes are #5 all-time for the Seahawks. He wore #7.

26. Linebacker from Colorado (1997-2004) who had been a 2nd round pick by the Steelers (1993-1996). He was a 2-time Pro Bowler for Seattle and he is a member of the Seahawk 35th Anniversary team. He made 107 starts for Seattle and his 48 sacks are #5 all-time for the Seahawks. He wore #94.

27. Seattle head coach (1983-1991) who compiled an 80-63 regular season record for the young franchise, with 3 post-season wins. He was also the head coach for the Rams (1973-1977 and 1992-1994) as well as the Bills (1978-1982). He is #3 all-time in wins for Seattle.

29. The first name of the player referred to in 15 ACROSS.

30. The first name of the player referred to in 11 ACROSS.

31. The first name of the player referred to in 24 DOWN.

32. The first name of the player referred to in 13 ACROSS.

33. Undrafted defensive tackle from Boston College (1982-1996) who only played for Seattle and is a member of the Seahawk 35th Anniversary team. He made 169 starts for Seattle and played in a franchise-record 218 games. He is #3 all-time for the Seahawks with 743 solo tackles and #6 with 48 sacks. He wore #72.

34. Quarterback from North Carolina State and Wisconsin (2012-2021) who has led the team to a pair of Super Bowls and one NFL Championship. He is the holder of all significant Seattle passing records and is even #5 in team history with 4,800 rushing yards! He wears #3.

36. The first name of the coach referred to in 14 ACROSS.

40. Quarterback from Alabama State (2011 and 2013-2015) who had been a 2nd round bust for the Vikings (2006-2010), going 10-10 as a starter but mainly excelling at handing off to Adrian Peterson. He was mostly a back-up in Seattle, with a 7-7 record as a starter. He wore #7.

41. 6'7" tight end from Miami (2015-2017) who had been a 3rd round pick by the Saints (2010-2014), for whom he was a 2-time Pro Bowler and the NFL leader with 16 scoring catches in 2013. He made two more Pro Bowls with Seattle, with 65 catches in 2016, before moving on to the Packers (2018-2019) and Bears (2020-2021). He wore #88.

44. 5' 10", 185-pound receiver/kick returner from Kansas State (2015-2021) who was a 3rd round pick and has only played for Seattle. He has had 3 straight seasons (2019-2021) with 1,000+ receiving yards and is #4 all-time for the Seahawks with 44 touchdown catches and #5 with 5,969 receiving yards. He wears #16.

45. The first name of the player referred to in 12 DOWN.

46. Quarterback from Notre Dame (1993-1996) who was taken 2nd overall by Seattle. He seemed to be growing in his first two seasons, but then hit a sudden and permanent plateau. He never made a Pro Bowl went 21-30 as a starter, with 76 interceptions against just 80 touchdown passes. He wore #3.

47. Offensive tackle from Oklahoma State (2010-2 015) who was a 1st round pick by Seattle. He was a 2012 Pro Bowler, made 72 career starts and played in two Super Bowls for the Seahawks, winning in 2014. He also went on to be a 2017 Pro Bowler with the Chargers (2017-2020). He wore #76.

50. Seattle head coach (1999-2008) who had earlier lead the Packers (1992-1998) to a pair of Super Bowls, winning in 1997. He took the Seahawks to their first Super Bowl in 2006, losing to the Steelers in a game in which the officials were "unkind". He had an 86-74 regular season record for Seattle and his 90 career wins are #2 for the franchise.

51. The first name of the player referred to in 16 DOWN.

52. Undrafted defensive back from Colgate (1985-1995) who was a 2-time Pro Bowler for Seattle. He led the NFL with 9 interceptions in 1993 and his 42 career interceptions are #2 in franchise history. He is also #1 for the Seahawks with 942 solo tackles. He went on to be a Super Bowl Champion with Green Bay in 1997. He wore #41.

55. Hall of Fame defensive tackle from Miami (1990-2000) who was taken 3rd overall and only played for Seattle. He was an 8-time Pro Bowler and the NFL Defensive Player of the Year in 1992. He is a member of the Seahawk Ring of Honor and his #96 has been retired by the team.

57. Running back from Notre Dame (1998-2001) who had been a 2nd round pick by the 49ers, for whom he was a 3-time Pro Bowler and a 1995 Super Bowl Champion. He made 2 more Pro Bowls with the Eagles (1995-1997) before coming to Seattle and rushing for 1,200+ yards twice (1999 and 2000). He wore #32.

59. Undrafted but aptly-named fullback from Georgia (1993-2007) who was a 2-time Pro Bowler and only played for Seattle. He had just 900 career rushing yards but was a ferocious lead blocker for 3 Seahawk backs who had 1,000-yard seasons. He also helped the team reach the 2006 Super Bowl. He wore #38.

60. The first name of the player referred to in 26 ACROSS.

61. The first name of the player referred to in 26 DOWN.

62. Quarterback from West Virginia who was a 2nd round pick by the Jets (2013-2016), for whom he went 33-30 as a starter. After being a back-up with the Giants (2017) and Chargers (2018), he came to Seattle and started 3 games in 2021 while the player referred to in 23 ACROSS was out with an injury. He wears #7.

63. 5'11" receiver from Miami (1988-1998) who was a 2nd round pick by Seattle. He only played for the Seahawks and was the NFL Man of the Year in 1995. He is a member of the 35th Anniversary team and is #2 all-time for the Seahawks in both catches (581) and receiving yards (7,620). He wore #89.

DOWN

2. Hall of Fame guard from Michigan (2001-2005) who was a 1st round pick by Seattle (2001-2005). He was a 3-time Pro Bowler for the Hawks and is a member of the NFL 2000s All-Decade Team. He started every game in 4 of his 5 seasons in Seattle and then went on to make 4 more Pro Bowls for Minnesota (2006-2011). He wore #76.

3. Defensive end from Purdue (2013-2017) who came to Seattle after having been a 3rd round pick by Detroit (2008-2012). With the Seahawks, he was a 2016 Pro Bowler and a member of two Super Bowl teams, winning in 2014. He had 35 sacks and 14 forced fumbles for Seattle. He wore #56.

4. Undrafted quarterback from Milton (Wisconsin, but now closed) (1980-1991) who was a 3-time Pro Bowler for Seattle and is a member of the Seahawk Ring of Honor. He is 3rd in franchise history in passing yardage (2 6,132) and 2nd in scoring passes (195). He went 70-49 as a starter for Seattle. He wore #17.

6. Undrafted, Hall of Fame defensive tackle/end from Texas A&M-Kingsville (2001-2003) who began with Minnesota (1990-2000). He made 7 career Pro Bowls, one with Seattle, and is a member of the NFL 100th Anniversary Team. He had 138 career sacks and was known for his scary, game-day face paint. He wore #93.

7. Running back from Alabama (2000-2007) who was a 1st round pick by Seattle and as 3-time Pro Bowler. He helped the team reach the 2006 Super Bowl, the same season in which he was the NFL MVP with 1,800 rushing yards and 27 rushing touchdowns. His 100 career rushing touchdowns are #1 for the Hawks. He wore #37.

8. Offensive tackle from Florida State (1997-2009) who was taken 6th overall and only played for Seattle. He was a 9-time Pro Bowler and helped the Seahawks make it to the 2006 Super Bowl. He is a member of the NFL 100th Anniversary Team and his #71 has been retired by the team.

SEATTLE SEAHAWKS

9. Undrafted defensive end from Texas A&M (2009 and 2013-2017) who was a 2-time Pro Bowler for Seattle and played in two Super Bowls, winning in 2014. He came back to the Seahawks after spending 2010-2012 in Tampa. His brother, Martellus, was a Pro Bowl tight end for the Bears. He wore #72.

12. Running back from Cal (2010-2015 and 2019) who had been a 1st round pick by the Bills (2007-2010). He made 4 Pro Bowls with Seattle and played in two Super Bowls. They would have won in 2015 also ....if he had been given the ball at the 2-yard line!! His 58 rushing touchdowns are #2 in franchise history. He wore #24.

17. Defensive back from Ohio State (1997-2003) who was taken 3rd overall by Seattle. He was a 1998 Pro Bowler and had 20 career interceptions for the Seahawks. He went on to play for Washington (2005-2008) and New England (2009). His dad, Ron, ran for 2,000 yards for Dallas (1979-1984). He wore #24.

18. Receiver from Ohio State (1995-1999) who was taken 7th overall by Seattle, for whom he had 3 years with 1,000+ receiving yards. He then went on to have 3 more 1,000-yard seasons with the Bucs. He is the only player in NFL history with 10,000 receiving yards who never made a Pro Bowl. He wore #84.

22. Seattle head coach (1995-1998) whose teams went 8-8, 7-9 and 8-8. He went on to lead the 49ers to losing records in 2003 and 2004. He had earlier built a reputation for excellence as a college coach, winning two National Championships with Miami (1989 and 1991).

23. Running back from Ferrum (Virginia) (1990-1997) who was a 4th round pick by Seattle and a 3-time Pro Bowler. He had 4 straight seasons with 1,000+ rushing yards for the Seahawks, with a career-best 1,545 yards in 1994. His 6,706 career rushing yards are #2 in franchise history and he is 4th in rushing scores (44). He wore #42.

24. Defensive back from Texas (2010-2018) who was a 1st round pick by Seattle, for whom he was a 6-time Pro Bowler. He played on those two now familiar Super Bowl teams and went on to make another Pro Bowl with the 2019 Ravens. He started every game in 6 straight seasons for "The Legion of BOOM". He wore #29.

26. Undrafted receiver from Stanford (2011-2018) who only played for Seattle and was a 2-time Pro Bowler. He also played in those two Super Bowls and lead the NFL with 14 touchdown catches in 2015. He had 1,000+ receiving yards in both 2015 and 2016 and is #3 in team history with 493 catches. He wore #15 and #89.

27. From 1976-1999, the Seahawks played their home games in the _____ Dome.

28. Undrafted kicker from North Carolina State (2011-2016) who first played for Baltimore (2008-2009) and Denver (2010). With Seattle, he played in those two Super Bowls before moving on to Buffalo (2017-2019). His 175 career field goals are the most in franchise history. He wore #4.

32. Defensive back from Virginia Tech (2010-2017) who was a 5th round pick and only played for Seattle. He was a 4-time Pro Bowler and played in those two Super Bowls. He teamed with the player referred to in 12 DOWN to make a terrific twosome at the safety position. A neck injury forced his retirement. He wore #31.

35. Linebacker from Utah State (2012-2021) who was a 2nd round pick and has only played for the Seahawks. He is a 7-time Pro Bowler and was huge for those two Super Bowl teams. He led the NFL in tackles twice (2016 and 2019) and he is #2 all-time for Seattle with 819 solo tackles. At age 31 he had a career-year in 2021. He wears #54.

37. The first name of the player referred to in 9 DOWN.

38. Bruising fullback from Florida (1986-1993) who was a 1st round pick by Seattle and a 2-time Pro Bowler. In addition to his 4,579 rushing yards (#6 in team history) he caught a remarkable 471 passes (4th most). He used the middle initial in his name. He wore #32.

39. Seattle head coach (2010-2021) who led Seattle to those two Super Bowls. His run of 9 straight winning 'seasons ended in 2021 and he is facing a rebuild for 2022.

40. The first name of the player referred to in 19 ACROSS.

42. The first name of the player referred to in 2 5 ACROSS.

43. Quarterback from Boston College (2001-2010) who had been a 6th round pick by the Packers (1998-2000). He was a 3-time Pro Bowler for Seattle and he led the team to the 2006 Super Bowl. He went 69-62 as a starter for the Hawks and is #2 in team history in passing yardage (29,434) and #3 in scoring passes (174). He wore #8.

48. Defensive back from Central Florida (2017-2020) who was a 3rd round pick by Seattle and a 2019 Pro Bowler. He had 6 interceptions in his time with the Seahawks before moving on to the dreadful Jaguars for 2021. He wore #26.

49. Undrafted kicker from UCLA (1982-1990) who is a member of the Seahawk 35th Anniversary team. His 159 field goals are #2 in team history. He went on to play for Atlanta (1991-1994) and Pittsburgh (1995-1998), amassing 366 field goals (18th in NFL history) over his 18 seasons.

53. Quarterback from Iowa State (2003-2009) who was a 4th round pick by Seattle. He was mainly a back-up and went 5-9 in his limited starting opportunities. He was pretty agile and is #8 in franchise history in both passing yardage (3,547) and touchdown passes (25). He wore #15.

54. Undrafted punter from Florida State (1991-19970 who was a 1994 Pro Bowler for Seattle and his 554 career punts are 2nd most in team history. He also played for the Eagles (1989), Bills (1990) and Rams (1998-1999). He died suddenly at age 52 while on vacation with his wife in Costa Rica. He wore #14.

56. The first name of the coach referred to in 11 DOWN.

58. The first name of the player referred to in 6 DOWN.

SEATTLE SEAHAWKS

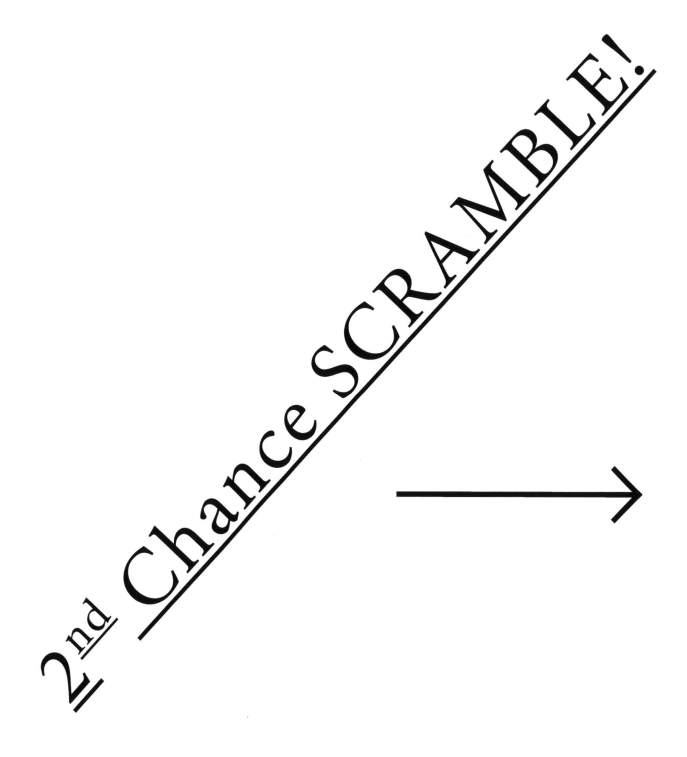

SEATTLE SEAHAWKS

ACROSS

1. EANHSRM ＿＿＿＿＿＿＿
5. FRUTNAT ＿＿＿＿＿＿＿
10. BNORNOSI ＿＿＿＿＿＿＿＿
11. EENOTSPR ＿＿＿＿＿＿＿＿
13. XAM ＿＿＿
14. VAED ＿＿＿＿
15. ACSNRO ＿＿＿＿＿＿
16. GNREU ＿＿＿＿＿
19. RNGEAM ＿＿＿＿＿＿
20. UUATTP ＿＿＿＿＿＿
21. RAENRW ＿＿＿＿＿＿
23. IGHTWR ＿＿＿＿＿＿
25. AKTIN ＿＿＿＿＿
26. BNOWR ＿＿＿＿＿
27. XONK ＿＿＿＿
29. JON ＿＿＿
30. FAOL ＿＿＿＿
31. AMK ＿＿＿
32. AHCD ＿＿＿＿
33. SNAH ＿＿＿＿
34. OISNWL ＿＿＿＿＿＿
36. HUCKC ＿＿＿＿＿
40. NSJCKAO ＿＿＿＿＿＿＿
41. AHRGMA ＿＿＿＿＿＿
44. KTTOECL ＿＿＿＿＿＿＿
45. ALER ＿＿＿＿
46. MREIR ＿＿＿＿＿
47. GNKOU ＿＿＿＿＿
50. HMRLGENO ＿＿＿＿＿＿＿＿
51. RSCIH ＿＿＿＿＿
52. SONRNBIO ＿＿＿＿＿＿＿＿
55. EKDNYNE ＿＿＿＿＿＿＿
57. AESRWTT ＿＿＿＿＿＿＿
59. TNOSGR ＿＿＿＿＿＿
60. SSLLRUE ＿＿＿＿＿＿＿
61. RONM ＿＿＿＿
62. MSTIH ＿＿＿＿＿
63. DSELAB ＿＿＿＿＿＿

DOWN

2. NOHCHSTNIU ＿＿＿＿＿＿＿＿＿＿
3. VRIAL ＿＿＿＿＿
4. KEGIR ＿＿＿＿＿
6. RDLNEA ＿＿＿＿＿＿
7. NAERAXELD ＿＿＿＿＿＿＿＿＿
8. OESJN ＿＿＿＿＿
9. ENBTEN ＿＿＿＿＿＿
12. LHCNY ＿＿＿＿＿
17. SGPRNIS ＿＿＿＿＿＿＿
18. LYAWGOAL ＿＿＿＿＿＿＿＿
22. SNOEKCIR ＿＿＿＿＿＿＿＿
23. RERNWA ＿＿＿＿＿＿
24. HOSMAT ＿＿＿＿＿＿
26. BLNDIAW ＿＿＿＿＿＿＿
27. IGKN ＿＿＿＿
28. CHHUAAKS ＿＿＿＿＿＿＿＿
32. ALNEHRLOCC ＿＿＿＿＿＿＿＿＿＿
35. GAWNER ＿＿＿＿＿＿
37. YJEO ＿＿＿＿
38. AIWMISLL ＿＿＿＿＿＿＿＿
39. LLRROCA ＿＿＿＿＿＿＿
40. JEO ＿＿＿
42. YETLR ＿＿＿＿＿
43. HLKCBSSEEA ＿＿＿＿＿＿＿＿＿＿
48. FFIGRNI ＿＿＿＿＿＿＿
49. NOHJOSN ＿＿＿＿＿＿＿
53. LAWLCAE ＿＿＿＿＿＿＿
54. NUTET ＿＿＿＿＿
56. DESNNI ＿＿＿＿＿＿
58. ASNUH ＿＿＿＿＿

XCIII

NEW YORK GIANTS

ACROSS

1. Wide-out from Michigan State (2005-2008) who had been a 1st round pick by Pittsburgh (2000-2004).c He had 2 years with 1,000+ receiving yards for the Giants and caught the winning touchdown pass in the final minute of the 2008 Super Bowl. He also managed to shoot himself in a New York club, thus ending his Giant career. He wore #17.

7. The first name of the coach referred to in 22 ACROSS.

8. Kicker from UCLA {1993-2000) who came to the Giants after playing for the Falcons, Bills and Broncos (1991-1992). He helped the 2000 team reach the Super Bowl and his 123 field goals are #2 in the history of the franchise. He wore #3.

9. The Giants beat the Bills in the 1991 Super Bowl, played in _____.

11. Running back from Georgia (1990-1997) who was 1st round pick and only played for the Giants. He was a 2-time Pro Bowler and a 1991 Super Bowl Champion. He had 5 straight seasons with 1,000+ rushing yards (1991-1995) and his 6,897 career rushing yards are #2 in team history. He wore #27.

12. Quarterback from Morehead State (1979-1993) who was a 1st round pick and only played for the Giants. He was a 2-time Super Bowl Champion (1987 and 1991), though he missed the 1991 game due to injury. He is a member of the team's Ring of Honor and is #2 all-time for the Giants in all passing categories. His #11 has been retired by the team.

14. Tight end from Mississippi (2017-2021) who was a 1st round pick by the Giants. He has exceeded 40 catches in each of his 5 seasons, with 64 catches in his rookie year and 63 in his 2020 Pro Bowl season. He wears #88.

16. Cornerback from Florida and North Alabama (2016-2019) who had been a 2nd round pick by the Rams (2012-2015). He was a 2016 Pro Bowler for the Giants and had 12 career interceptions for New York, 2 of which he returned for scores. Late in 2019 he got in trouble on Twitter and was cut. He has since played for the Saints and Titans. He wore #20.

19. The first name of the player referred to in 1 ACROSS.

20. Hall of Fame defensive end from North Carolina (1981-1993) who was a 1st round pick and only played for the Giants. He was a 10-time Pro Bowler and a 3-time NFL Defensive Player of the Year. He was also a 2-time Super Bowl Champion (1987 and 1991). He wore #56.

22. Punter from Miami (2003-2009) who came to the Giants after 15 seasons with the Patriots, Eagles, Cardinals and Sea hawks (1988-2002). He ended his career with New York, for whom he was a 2008 Super Bowl Champion and a 2008 Pro Bowler. His 1,713 punts over 22 seasons are the most in NFL history. He wore #18.

25. The first name of a linebacker from Michigan State (1984-1992) who was a 5th round pick by the Giants. He was a 2-time Super Bowl Champion for New York (1987 and 1991) and then went on to play for Washington and Cleveland. He is a member of the team's Ring of Honor and the NFL 1980s All-Decade Team. He wore #58.

26. Wide-out from North Carolina (2009-2013 and 2015}, who was a 1st round pick by the Giants and a 2012 Super Bowl Champion. He had 2 years with 1,000+ receiving yards for New York and an incredible post-season for those Super Bowl Champs, finishing with 10 catches in the Super Bowl win over New England. He wore #88.

28. Tight end from Notre Dame (1985-1990) who was a 4th round pick by the Giants, for whom he was a 2-time Pro Bowler and a 2-time Super Bowl Champion (1987 and 1991). He had 1,000 receiving yards in 1986 and he is also a member of the team's Ring of Honor. His blocking skill, reliable hands and heart made him a fan favorite. He wore #89.

30. The first name of the plater referred to in 32 DOWN.

31. Wide-out from LSU (2014-2018) who was 1st round pick by the Giants, the 2014 NFL Offensive Rookie of the Year and a 3-time Pro Bowler. He had 4 seasons with 1,000+ receiving yards for New York before a controversial trade sent him to Cleveland, for whom he had another 1,000-yard season in 2019. He is now with the Rams (2021). He wore #13.

32. Quarterback from Duke (1992-1997) who was a 1st round pick by the Giants and an immense disappointment. He went 23-30 as a starter with only 40 touchdown passes against 49 interceptions. He went on to succeed in the investment world with several prestigious New York firms. He wore #17.

35. Undrafted center from Rutgers (2004-2010) who came to the Giants from the Browns (2000-2003). He was a 3-time Pro Bowler for the Giants and a 2008 Super Bowl Champion. He started every game in 3 straight seasons for New York (2007-2009) and is now an analyst for the NFL Network. He is also known for his philanthropy. He wore #60.

42. Safety from Clemson (1983-1989) who was a 2nd round pick by the Giants, for whom he was a 1987 Super Bowl Champion and a 1988 Pro Bowler. He made 100 starts for New York, including every game in 3 of his 7 seasons, with 27 career interceptions. He wore #43.

43. Guard from Boston College (1996-2001) who had been a 4th round pick by Dallas (1993-1995) and a 2-time Super Bowl Champion (1994 and 1996). He was a 2-time Pro Bowler for the Giants and went on to make a 3rd Pro Bowl with the 49ers (2002). He started 92 out of a possible 96 regular season games for New York. He wore #65.

44. Wide-out from Florida (1997-2004) who was a 1st round pick by the Giants and helped the team reach the 2001 Super Bowl. He had 368 catches for New York and though he never had a 1,000-yard season or made a Pro Bowl, he was an excellent route runner with reliable hands. He wore #88.

46. New York coach (1993-1996) whose first team went 11-5 but his other teams slipped to 9-7 and 5-11. He had earlier guided Denver (1981-1992) to 3 Super Bowl appearances and a 110-73 regular season record. Later, with Atlanta (1997-2003) he made it to a 4th Super Bowl.

47. The first name of the player referred to in 19 ACROSS.

48. The first name of the player referred to in 29 ACROSS.

51. Hall of Fame defensive end from Texas Southern (1993-2007) who was a 2nd round pick and only played for the Giants. He was a 7-time Pro Bowler and a 2-time NFL sacks leader. He was also the 2001 NFL Defensive Player of the Year and a 2008 Super Bowl Champion. He has gone on to become a successful media personality. He wore #92.

53. Both Peyton and Eli Manning attended a prestigious, private New Orleans high school called Isidore _____.

56. Tight end from Miami (2002-2007) who was a 1st round pick, a 4-time Pro Bowler and a 2008 Super Bowl Champion for the Giants (though he missed the game due to a Week 15 injury). He later became a Super Bowl Champion again with the Saints in 2010. His 371 catches are #5 all-time for New York. He wore #80.

57. The first name of the coach referred to in 12 DOWN.

58. Wide-out from Michigan (1996-2008) who was a 2nd round pick and only played for the Giants. He was a 2008 Super Bowl Champion and, though he never made a Pro Bowl, is #1 alltime for New York in catches (668), receiving yardage (9,497) and touchdown catches (54). He wore #89 and #81.

60. Undrafted kicker from Michigan (2005-2006) who first played for Atlanta (2001-2004), for whom he led the NFL in field goals with 35 in 2002. He was a 2005 Pro Bowler for the Giants when he had a career-best 35 field goals. He now does color and sideline work for CBS. He wore #2.

62. Kicker from Mexico (1986-1991) who was undrafted out of Texas. He came to the Giants after playing for the Colts (1983-1985). He was a 1987 Super Bowl Champion for New York but did not appear in New York's 1991 Super Bowl win due to injury. He wore #2.

66. Quarterback from Duke (2019-2011) who was a 1st round pick and taken 6th overall by the Giants. His selection was not popular with the fan base and he has not exactly distinguished himself on the field. His record as a starter is just 12-25 but in fairness, he hasn't had a lot of help. It seems unlikely that he will be "the guy" the team hoped he would be. He wears #8.

67. The first name of the player referred to in 2 ACROSS.

68. Wide-out from Michigan State (1987-1992) who was a 1st round pick and a 1991 Super Bowl Champion for the Giants. He went on to play for the Dolphins, Packers and Eagles. He did a 7-year stretch for fraud and money laundering and he is the father of a Heisman Trophy winner. He wore #82.

70. The first name of the player referred to in 37 ACROSS.

71. The first name of the player referred to in 32 ACROSS.

72. Receiver from USC (2007-2010) who was a 2nd round pick by the Giants, a 2008 Super Bowl Champion and a 2009 Pro Bowler. 2009 was his only fully healthy season and he set a team record with 107 catches. He had 48 catches in 2010 before finishing with 2-more injury-filled seasons elsewhere. He wore #12.

73. The first name of the coach referred to in 26 DOWN.

74. Quarterback from Penn State (1999-2003) who had been a 1st round pick by Carolina (1995-1998). He led the Giants to the 2001 Super Bowl and then went on to play for the Raiders, Titans and Colts (2004-2010). His 1,447 completions are #3 all-time for New York. He has been bravely candid about his struggle with alcoholism. He wore #5.

75. Running back from Penn State (2018-2021) who is a Bronx native and was taken 2nd overall by the Giants. He was the NFL Rookie of the Year and a 2018 Pro Bowler when he rushed for 1,300 yards with 91 catches. He had another 1,000-yard season in 2019 but played in just 2 games in 2020 due to injury. 2021 has also been a struggle. He wears #26.

DOWN

1. Running back from Marshall (2007-2012) who was 2nd round pick by the Giants and a 2-time Super Bowl Champion (2008 and 2012). He had two years in New York with 1,000+ rushing yards and he is 6th all-time for the Giants with 4,232 career rushing yards. He finished up with the Colts (2013-2015). He wore #44.

2. New York coach (2018-2019) whose teams went just 5-11 and 4-12. He had earlier been the Cleveland head coach (2011-2012) and those teams also went only 4-12 and 5-11. He has gone on to serve as the Denver offensive coordinator (2020-2021).

3. Quarterback from West Virginia (1984-1992) who was a 3rd round pick, a 2-time Super Bowl Champion and a 1994 Pro Bowler for New York. He didn't play in the 1997 rout of Denver but did lead the Giants to a dramatic win in 1991 over Buffalo. He was mainly a backup with New York but he did go 16-9 in his regular season starts. He wore #15.

4. The first name of the coach referred to in 2 DOWN.

5. 6'4", 265-pound running back from Auburn and Southern Illinois (2005-2011 and 2013) who was a 4th round pick by the Giants and a 2-time Super Bowl Champion (2008 and 2012). He had 2 seasons with 1,000+ rushing yards for New York and his 60 rushing touchdowns are the most in franchise history. He wore #22.

6. Running back from Virginia (1997-2006) who was a 2nd pick and a 3-time Pro Bowler. He only played for the Giants and helped the team make it to the 2001 Super Bowl. He is in New York's Ring of Honor and his 10,449 career rushing yards

XCVI

are #1 in franchise history. He is now a national media presence. He wore #21.

10. The first name of the player referred to in 30 ACROSS.

13. The first name of the player referred to in 14 ACROSS.

51. Safety from Miami (2010-2014) who had been a 1st round pick by the Cardinals (2005-2009). He was a 2-time Pro Bowler for the Giants and a 2012 Super Bowl Champion. He had 26 career interceptions, 14 of them for New York. He wore #26.

17. Cornerback from Arizona State (1992-1999) who was a 2nd round pick by the Giants. He had 22 interceptions for New York and his most unusual first name is a reference to an early Christian community in Greece to whom St. Paul addressed several epistles. He wore #22.

19. Wide-out from Michigan (1992-1998) who had been 4th round pick by Pittsburgh (1990-1991). He never made a Pro Bowl or had a 1,000 yard season but had a skill set and productive career similar to the player referred to in 20 ACROSS. He is in the top 10 all-time for the Giants both in catches (334) and receiving yards (4,710). He wore #80.

21. The first name of the player referred to in 17 ACROSS.

22. San Diego State grad and New York defensive coordinator (1997-2001) who helped the 2000 team reach the Super Bowl. He went on to win 141 NFL games as the head coach for Carolina (2002-2010), Denver (2011-2014) and Chicago (2015-2017).

23. Running back from Miami (1986-1992) who had been a 1st round pick by the Cardinals (1979-1986), for whom he had 5 seasons with 1,000+ rushing yards. He was a 2-time Super Bowl Champion with the Giants (1987 and 1991) and was the MVP of the 1991 win. He wore #24.

24. The first name of the player referred to in 40 ACROSS.

25. New York head coach (2004-2015) who had earlier taken Jacksonville to the AFC Title Game in the team's 2nd year of existence and did so again 3 years later. With the Giants he was a 2-time Super Bowl Champion (2008 and 2012) and his 102 regular season wins are the 2nd most in franchise history. He is also a member of the Giants Ring of Honor.

27. In the 2000 NFC Championship Game, the Giants humiliated a _____ team by a score of 41-0.

29. The first name of the player referred to in 1 DOWN.

33. Defensive back from LSU (2005-2013) who was a 2nd round pick and only played for the Giants. He was a 2-time Super Bowl Champion (2008 and 2012) and appeared in 120 games for New York, 93 of them starts. He recorded 20 career interceptions and wore #23.

36. On their way to the 2008 Super Bowl, the Giants beat _____ in the divisional round by a score of 21-17.

37. The first name of the player referred to in 5 DOWN.

38. Punter from Towson (1985-1993 and 2006) who came to the Giants from the USFL. He was a 2-time Pro Bowler for New York and a 2-time Super Bowl Champion (1987 and 1991). He is a member of the NFL All-Decade Teams for both the 1980s and 1990s and is also a member of the Giants Hall of Fame. He wore #5.

39. Linebacker from Ohio State (1986-1992) who was a 2nd round pick by the Giants, a 1990 Pro Bowler and a 2-time Super Bowl Champion (1987 and 1991). He later made another Pro Bowl with the Browns (1994) and finished up with the Jets (1997-1998). His real first name is Thomas but he went by a nickname. Looking for his last name. He wore #52.

XCVII

40. Disgraced, wife beating kicker from Nebraska (2013-2016) who had been a 7th round pick by Seattle (2003-2007). He came to New York after playing for the Rams (2008-2011) and Bengals (2012). He was a 2015 Pro Bowler for the Giants, for who he had 77 career field goals. Now he speaks out openly against domestic violence. He wore #3.

41. Center from BYU (1985-1993) who came to the Giants after 3 years in the USFL. He was a 3-time Pro Bowler and 2-time Super Bowl Champion for New York (1987 and 1991). He went on to make two more Pro Bowls with the 49ers and in 1985, became a Super Bowl Champion for a 3rd time. He wore #65.

45. Wide-out from Syracuse (2003-2008) who was a 6th round pick by the Giants and a 2006 Pro Bowler as a special teamer. He caught just 54 passes for New York but will always be revered for an amazing catch late in the 2008 Super Bowl that helped ruin New England's bid for a perfect season. He is now the team's Director of Player Personnel. He wore #85.

49. New York head coach (2016-2017) who had earlier been the team's offensive coordinator (2014-2015). His 2016 squad went 11-5 and won the NFC East but the 2017 season was plagued by injuries and suspensions. He was fired after the Giants had plunged to 2-10.

50. Linebacker from Miami (1993-2001) who, though just an 8th round pick by the Giants, was still a 5-time Pro Bowler. He helped New York reach the 2001 Super Bowl and is a member of the team's Ring of Honor. He started every game for 6 straight seasons (1996-2001) and is now a special assistant for the Giants. He wore #98.

52. Defensive end from Notre Dame (2005-2013) who was a 3rd round pick by the Giants, a 2- time Pro Bowler and a 2-time Super Bowl Champion (2008 and 2012). In the 2008 Super Bowl, he sacked Tom Brady twice and forced a crucial fumble. He is a member of the team's Ring of Honor and he wore #91.

54. Undrafted linebacker from Arizona (2005-2009) who came to the Giants from Washington (2001-2004). In New York he was a 2006 Pro Bowler and a 2008 Super Bowl Champion. He started every game in 3 straight seasons. A Compton escapee, he has done a lot of inner city work in LA with at-risk kids. He is now the DC at Arizona State. He wore #58.

55. Defensive back from Alabama (2015-2018) who was a 2nd round pick and a 3-time Pro Bowler for the Giants. He started 59 out of a possible 64 regular season games for New York before moving on to sign a massive contract with Washington (2019 2021), for whom he has made another 35 starts. He wore #21.

59. Running back/kick returner from Towson (1989-1994) who was a 5th round pick by the Giants and a 1991 Super Bowl Champion. He later helped the Patriots reach the 1997 Super Bowl but is now doing a 30-year prison term for burglary and sex crimes. He wore #30 but now wears #14782."

61. 5'7" running back from Syracuse (1982-1989) who was a 2nd round pick by the Giants, a 2- time Pro Bowler and a 1987 Super Bowl Champion. He had 3 seasons with 1,000+ rushing yards for New York and his 5,296 career rushing yards are the 3rd most in franchise history. He wore #20.

63. On their way to the 2001 Super Bowl, the Giants beat the _____ in the divisional round by a score of 20-10.

64. Giants head coach (1997-2003) who was the 1997 NFL Coach of the Year and also led the team to the 2001 Super Bowl. A 4-12 record in 2003 got him fired but he went on to be the offensive coordinator for the Ravens (2005-2006). He died of a heart attack in June 2021 at age 71.

65. Offensive lineman from Illinois (2003-2013) who was a 5th round pick, a 2009 Pro Bowler and a 2-time Super Bowl Champion for the Giants (2008 and 2012). He made 160 regular season starts for New York, including every game in 7 straight seasons (2003-2009). He wore #66.

69. The Giants were founded and have always been run by members of the _____ family.

NEW YORK GIANTS

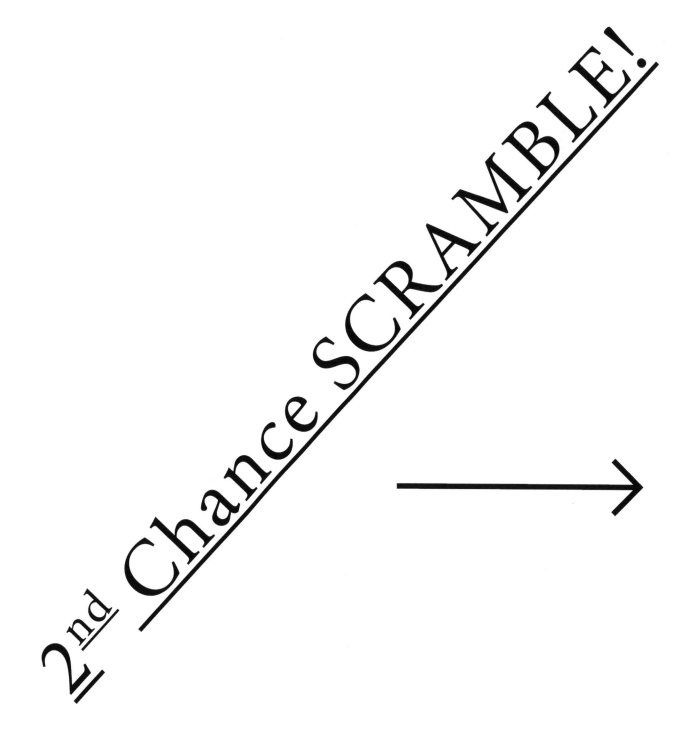

2nd Chance SCRAMBLE!

NEW YORK GIANTS

ACROSS

1. URSBERS ___ ___ ___ ___ ___ ___ ___

7. DNA ___ ___ ___

8. IOUSADL ___ ___ ___ ___ ___ ___ ___

9. APMAT ___ ___ ___ ___ ___

11. OAHMPTN ___ ___ ___ ___ ___ ___ ___

12. SMISM ___ ___ ___ ___ ___

14. AMENRG ___ ___ ___ ___ ___ ___

16. NNEISJK ___ ___ ___ ___ ___ ___ ___

19. LCXIPOA ___ ___ ___ ___ ___ ___ ___

20. LOAYRT ___ ___ ___ ___ ___ ___

22. SLEEGFA ___ ___ ___ ___ ___ ___ ___

25. LCRA ___ ___ ___ ___

26. NKICS ___ ___ ___ ___ ___

28. ARVOAB ___ ___ ___ ___ ___ ___

30. EOJ ___ ___ ___

31. EHBKMAC ___ ___ ___ ___ ___ ___ ___

32. NBORW ___ ___ ___ ___ ___

35. HOARA ___ ___ ___ ___ ___

42. NRIKDA ___ ___ ___ ___ ___ ___

43. TOENS ___ ___ ___ ___ ___

44. LRIAIDHL ___ ___ ___ ___ ___ ___ ___ ___

46. SVEEER ___ ___ ___ ___ ___ ___

47. TRYRE ___ ___ ___ ___ ___

48. INMAA ___ ___ ___ ___ ___

51. NTRAASH ___ ___ ___ ___ ___ ___ ___

53. NWMNAE ___ ___ ___ ___ ___ ___

56. ESOHYKC ___ ___ ___ ___ ___ ___ ___

57. OTM ___ ___ ___

58. MOOERT ___ ___ ___ ___ ___ ___

60. EFYEL ___ ___ ___ ___ ___

62. LARGEEL ___ ___ ___ ___ ___ ___ ___

66. NEJSO ___ ___ ___ ___ ___

67. BDAR ___ ___ ___ ___

68. AMGINR ___ ___ ___ ___ ___ ___

70. VETSE ___ ___ ___ ___ ___

71. ARUL ___ ___ ___ ___

72. MHTSI ___ ___ ___ ___ ___

73. NEB ___ ___ ___

74. OCLLINS ___ ___ ___ ___ ___ ___ ___

75. ABLEKYR ___ ___ ___ ___ ___ ___ ___

DOWN

1. SRWABHDA ___ ___ ___ ___ ___ ___ ___ ___

2. UURHSRM ___ ___ ___ ___ ___ ___ ___

3. TROETELHS ___ ___ ___ ___ ___ ___ ___ ___ ___

4. TAP ___ ___ ___

5. JOBASC ___ ___ ___ ___ ___ ___

6. EARBRB ___ ___ ___ ___ ___ ___

10. NDILEA ___ ___ ___ ___ ___ ___

13. AMRK ___ ___ ___ ___

15. OLREL ___ ___ ___ ___ ___

17. PKRSSA ___ ___ ___ ___ ___ ___

19. ALYCWLOA ___ ___ ___ ___ ___ ___ ___ ___

21. DOELL ___ ___ ___ ___ ___

22. XFO ___ ___ ___

23. NARSDNOE ___ ___ ___ ___ ___ ___ ___ ___

24. ARKM ___ ___ ___ ___

25. UCLHGINO ___ ___ ___ ___ ___ ___ ___ ___

27. IINKVG ___ ___ ___ ___ ___ ___

29. DHAMA ___ ___ ___ ___ ___

33. ERTWBSE ___ ___ ___ ___ ___ ___ ___

36. LALSDA ___ ___ ___ ___ ___ ___

37. ITIK ___ ___ ___ ___

38. EDAANTL ___ ___ ___ ___ ___ ___ ___

39. SHNONJO ___ ___ ___ ___ ___ ___ ___

40. NWBOR ___ ___ ___ ___ ___

41. STEOA ___ ___ ___ ___ ___

45. TEEYR ___ ___ ___ ___ ___

49. CDMOAO ___ ___ ___ ___ ___ ___

50. ARAMDEST ___ ___ ___ ___ ___ ___ ___ ___

52. CTUK ___ ___ ___ ___

54. EEPRCI ___ ___ ___ ___ ___ ___

55. CNLLSOI ___ ___ ___ ___ ___ ___ ___

59. ETGGEMT ___ ___ ___ ___ ___ ___ ___

61. RSIOMR ___ ___ ___ ___ ___ ___

63. EAESLG ___ ___ ___ ___ ___ ___

64. SALFSE ___ ___ ___ ___ ___ ___

65. IELHD ___ ___ ___ ___ ___

69. RMAA ___ ___ ___ ___

CI

ACROSS

1. Packer head coach (2006-2018) whose team won the 2011 Super Bowl. He went 125-77-2 in the regular season (the 2nd most wins in franchise history) and 108 in the playoffs. Friction with Aaron Rodgers was instrumental in his firing. He has been named head coach for the Cowboys for 2020.

4. Running back from Florida State (1992-1997) who was a 4th round pick and is a 1997 Super Bowl Champion. He also helped the team reach the 1998 Super Bowl and he is a member of the Packer Hall of Fame. He ran for 3,300 yards for the Packers and was the team's offensive coordinator (2015-2017). He wore #34.

8. Undrafted free agent fullback from Shippensburg (2007-2015) who was a 3-time Pro Bowler and is a 2011 Super Bowl Champion. He gained just 601 rushing yards but was a fierce blocker, able receiver and solid special teamer. He began with the Steelers (2005-2006) and is also a 2006 Super Bowl Champ. He wore #30.

9. Tight end from Boston College (1992-1999) who was a 6th round pick and only played for the Packers. He was a 3-time Pro Bowler and is a 1997 Super Bowl Champion. He also helped Green Bay make it to the 198 Super Bowl. He is a member of the Packer Hall of Fame. He wore #89.

11. Receiver from Alcorn State (1999-2012) who was a 7th round pick and only played for the Packers. He was a 4-time Pro Bowler and is a 2011 Super Bowl Champion. He is the all-time franchise leader in both catches (743) and receiving yards (10,137). His 61 scoring catches rank 4th all-time. He wore #80.

12. Defensive back from Iowa (2013-2016) who was a 5th round pick by the Packers. He had 8 interceptions for the Packers plus 3 touch downs on punt returns. He has since gone on to the Bills (2017-2019) for whom he was a 2017 Pro Bowler. He wore #33.

13. The first name of the player referred to in 29 DOWN.

14. Disgraced defensive back from William and Mary (1997-2004) who was a 2nd round pick by the Packers and is a 1997 Super Bowl Champion. He also helped the team reach the 1998 Super Bowl. He was a 2-time. Pro Bowler with the Packers and his 36 interceptions are 6th most in franchise history. He wore #42.

15. Linebacker from USC (2012-2018) who was a 1st round pick and only played for the Packers. He was often injured and made just 48 starts in his 7 seasons, with no Pro Bowl appearances. In view of his lofty draft status, he has to be seen as something of a disappointment. He wore #53.

16. Receiver from South Carolina (1988-1994) who was a

21. Defensive back from Florida State (1990-2001) who was a 2nd round pick and only played for the Packers, for whom he was a 4-time Pro Bowler. He is a 1997 Super Bowl Champion who also helped the team make it to the 1998 Super Bowl. He is a member of the Packer Hall of Fame. He wore #36.

22. Defensive end from North Carolina (2014-2016) who had been a 1st round pick by the Panthers (2002-2009) and taken 2nd overall. He then moved on to the Bears (2010-2013) before coming to Green Bay. He had 60 career sacks and 9 Pro Bowl appearances; one with the Packers. He wore #56.

24. Brett Favre had been a 2nd round pick by _____.

26. Aaron Rodgers is a native of _____, California.

28. Defensive tackle from Kansas (1993-1999 & 2000-2003) who had been a 3rd round pick by the Vikings but never played for them. He played only for the Packers and is a 1997 Super Bowl Champion. He also helped the team reach the 1998 Super Bowl. He was a massive run-stopper. He wore #93.

31. Tight end from Miami (2000-2007) who was a 1st round pick and a 3-time Pro-Bowler for Green Bay. Only one Packer tight end (Paul Coffman) had more than his 256 catches and 32 scoring receptions. He made 94 career starts for the Packers before moving on to the Jets (2008). His real first name is Daniel. He wore #88.

32. Heisman Trophy-winning receiver/returner from Michigan (1996 & 1999) who had been a 1st round pick by the Redskins (1992-1994). He helped the Packers win the 1997 Super Bowl by returning a kickoff for a touchdown and he was the MVP of the game. He never developed into a skilled receiver however. He wore #81.

34. Defensive end from Iowa (2002-2009) who was a 5th round pick by the Packers and a 2-time Pro Bowler. He started every game for the Packers in 3 straight seasons (2004-2006) and did so again in 2008. He had 54 sacks for the Packers before finishing up with 2 injury-plagued seasons with the Jags. He wore #74.

36. Receiver from San Jose State (2007-2013 & 2015) who was a 3rd round pick by the Packers and is a 2011 Super Bowl Champion. He led the NFL with 14 touchdown catches in 2012. His 45 career scoring catches are 9th most in franchise history. He caught 73 balls for the 2014 Raiders. He wore #89.

38. Kicker from Colorado (2007-2019) who was a 6th round pick and has only played for the Packers. He led the NFL in scoring in 2007 and is a 2011 Super Bowl Champion. His 329 career field goals are the most in team history. He wears #2.

40. Undrafted defensive back from Louisiana Tech (2006-2014 & 2018-2019) who has been a one-time Pro Bowler for the Packers and is a 2011 Super Bowl Champion. His 30 career interceptions are 10th most in franchise history. He spent 2015-2017 with the Browns and Cardinals. He has always worn #38.

42. Offensive tackle from Tennessee (2000-2011) who was a 2nd round pick and only played for the Packers. He was a 2-time Pro Bowler and is a 2011 Super Bowl Champion. He started every game in 3 straight seasons (2003-2005) and did so again in 2007 and 2010. He made 160 career starts and wore #76.

43. The first name of the player referred to in 19 ACROSS.

44. The first name of the player referred to in 27 ACROSS.

48. The first name of the player referred to in 6 ACROSS.

50. Kicker from El Paso, Texas (1989-1996) who was a 6th round pick by the Packers and is a 1997 Super Bowl Champion. He is a member of the Packer Hall of Fame and his 173 field goals are the 3rd most in franchise history. He kicked another 29 field goals for Arizona (1998-1999). He wore #13.

53. Undrafted kicker from Cal (1997-2005) who helped the Packers make it to the 1998 Super Bowl and is a member of the Packer Hall of Fame. His 226 field goals are 2nd most in Packer history. He went on to play for Minnesota (2006-2011) and his 135 field goals there are also 2nd most in team history. He wore #8.

55. Running back from Alabama (2013-2016) who was a 2nd round pick, he NFC Offensive Rookie other Year and a 2013 Pro Bowler. Injuries and weight concerns ended his run in Green Bay. After a forgettable year in Seattle (2017), he retired at age 27. His 3,435 rushing yards are 10th most in Packer history. He wore #27.

56. Packer head coach (2000-2005) whose teams went 57-39 with 3 division titles. His post-season record, however, was just 2-4. He went on to post a 25-25 record as head coach at Texas A&M (2008-2011). His last NFL job was as the Miami offensive coordinator (2012-2013).

60. Undrafted running back from Notre Dame (2007-2011) who came to the Packers from the Giants (2005-2006). He was a 2009 Pro Bowler and is a 2011 Super Bowl Champion. He had two years with 1,200+ rushing yards (2008-2009) and his 4,143 career yards are 5th all-time in Packer history. He wore #25.

61. The first name of the player referred to in 32 ACROSS.

62. The first name of the player referred to in 28 ACROSS.

63. Hall of Fame and noted homophobe from Tennessee (1993-1998) who had earlier starred for the Eagles (1985-1992). He was a 1997 Super Bowl Champion and a 6-time Pro Bowler with the Packers. He was also a two-time NFL Defensive Player of the Year. He died from heart trouble at age 43. He wore #92.

DOWN

1. Linebacker from USC (2009-2018) who was a 1st round pick by the Packers, a 6 time Pro Bowler and a 2011 Super Bowl Champion. He made 137 starts for the Packers and recorded 84 sacks before going to the Rams (2019). His dad was a 4-time Pro Bowl linebacker with the Falcons and Browns (1978-1996). He wore #52.

2. Quarterback from UCLA (2015-2017) who was a 5th round pick by the Packers. He started 9 games in 2017 when Aaron Rodgers got hurt in Minnesota and played well in spots, despite going just 3-6. He didn't get into a game with the 2018 Seahawks but did attempt 11 passes with the 2019 Cardinals. He wore #7.

3. Receiver from Virginia Tech (1995- 2001) who was a 3rd round pick by the Packers, a one-time Pro Bowler and a 1997 Super Bowl Champion. He also helped the Packers reach the 1998 Super Bowl. He was the 1998 NFL leader in receiving yards and he is a member of the Packer Hall of Fame. He wore #86.

4. Defensive back from Florida State (1992-1994) who was a Jim Thorpe winner at FSU and a 1st round pick by the Packers. After leaving the Packers, he played 11 more seasons with 5 other teams, most notably the Dolphins. He is the only player in NFL history with 50 interceptions and no Pro Bowls appearances. He wore #27.

5. Packer head coach (1992-1998) who compiled a 75-37 regular season record and took the team to two Super Bowls (1997 & 1998), winning in 1998. He moved on to be the head man in Seattle (1999-2008), where he went 86-74 and took the team to its first Super Bowl in 2006.

6. Guard from Penn State (1996-2004) who was a 6th round pick by the Packers, a 3-time Pro Bowler and a 1997 Super Bowl Champion. He also helped the team reach the 1998 Super Bowl. He is a member of the packer Hall of Fame. He started every game for the Packers in 6 straight seasons (1999-2004). He wore #62.

10. Receiver from Fresno State (2014-2019) who was a 2nd round pick, has only played for the Packers and is a 3-time Pro Bowler, to date. He had a career-best 1,386 receiving yards in 2018 and his 431 catches are 9th most in franchise history. His 44 touchdown catches are 10th most. He wears #17.

15. Linebacker from Northern Iowa (1990-1994) who was a 6th round pick by the Packers and a one-time Pro Bowler. With the Bills (1995-1997) he made 3 more Pro Bowls and was the NFL sacks leader and NFL Defensive Player of the Year in 1995. He finished up with the Jaguars and Vikings (1998-2000). He wore #95.

17. Defensive back from Texas A&I (2003-2010) who had been 6th round pick by Tampa (1997). He was with the Eagles (1998-2002) before coming to the Packers and making two Pro Bowls (2007 & 2008). He started every game for Green Bay in 5 straight seasons (2003-2007) and had 14 interceptions. He wore #31.

18. Running back from Georgia Tech (1994-2001) who was a 5th round pick by the Packers and a one-time Pro Bowler. He is a Super Bowl Champion

(1997} and a member of the Packer Hall of Fame. He also helped the team make it to the 1998 Super Bowl. His 3,937 rushing yards are 6th most in team history. He wore #35.

19. The first name of the player referred to in 16 ACROSS.

20. The first name of the player referred to in 24 DOWN.

21. Linebacker from Oregon State (2003-2010) who was a 1st round pick by the Packers and a 2011 Super Bowl Champion. He made 107 starts for the Packers and started every game in 4 different seasons. He moved on to Buffalo (2011-2012) and finished up with Washington (2013). He wore #5.

23. Guard from Central Florida (2008-2015) who was a 4th round pick by the Packers,3-time Pro Bowler and a 2011 Super Bowl Champion. He started every game in 6 of his 8 seasons in Green Bay then went on to make a Pro Bowl with the 2016 Bears. He wore #71.

25. Running back from El Paso, Texas (2017-2019) who was just a 5th round pick but emerged as a star in 2019. He tied for the most rushing touchdowns in the NFL in 2019 with 16 and also had a career-best 1,084 rushing yards. He wears #33.

27. Receiver from Kentucky (2011-2018) who was a 2nd round pick by the Packers and a 2014 Pro Bowler when he had a career-best 1,287 receiving yards. His 470 catches are 6th most in franchise history. He went on to the Cowboys for 2019. He wore #18.

28. Receiver from South Carolina (1992-1998) who was a 3rd round pick by the Packers. He is a 1997 Super Bowl Champion and was a member of the 1998 Super Bowl squad. He teamed with Brett Favre on a 99-yard scoring play in a Monday night win over the Bears and popularized the "Lambeau Leap". He wore #87.

29. Running back from Buffalo (2010-2016) who was a 6th round pick, only played for the Packers and was a member of the 2011 Super Bowl

Championship team, for whom he had 315 post-season rushing yards. He was noted for his versatility, recording 2,500 rushing yards and 1,000 receiving yards. He wore #44.

30. Running back from Nebraska (2000-2006 & 2009) who had been a 3rd round pick by Seattle. With the Packers, he was a 4-time Pro-Bowler and the 2003 NFC Offensive Player of the Year. He had 6 years for the Packers with 1,000+ rushing yards and his 8,322 career yards are the most in Packer history. He wore #30.

33. Heisman Trophy-winning and NFL Hall of Fame defensive back from Michigan (2006-2012) who had been a 1st round pick by Oakland. With the Packers he was a 4-time Pro Bowler and a 2011 Super Bowl Champion. He holds the Packer record with 9 interceptions returned for touchdowns. He wore #21.

35. Linebacker from Stanford (2016-2019) who was a 4th round pick by the Packers. He tied for the league lead with 144 tackles in 2017 and he exceeded that number in both 2018 and 2019. He started every game over the past 3 seasons. He wears #50.

36. The first name of the player referred to in 14 ACROSS.

37. Brett Favre played college football at Southern
_____.

39. Offensive tackle from Iowa (2010-2019) who was a 1st round pick and has only played for the Packers. He is a 2011 Super-Bowl Champion and has made 111 career starts, making every start in both 2016 and 2019. He wears #75.

41. Quarterback from Virginia (1987-1992) who was a 10th round pick by the Packers. He had one magic, Pro Bowl year in Green Bay in 1989 but injuries blighted his remaining years with the Packers. He finished up with 4 years as a back-up with the Colts and Lions. He wore #7.

CV

45. Undrafted free agent defensive back from Miami (2010-2016) who was a onetime Pro Bowler and 2011 Super Bowl Champion. He had 18 interceptions for the Packers. After sitting out 2017 due to concussion problems he helped the Rams reach the 2019 Super Bowl, mainly as a special teamer. He wore #37.

46. Receiver from Kansas State (2008-2017) who was a 2nd round pick by the Packers, a 2011 Super Bowl Champion and a 2014 Pro Bowler. He had 4 years for the Packers with 1,200+ receiving yards and his 69 scoring catches are 2nd most in franchise history. He spent 2018 with the Raiders, then retired. He wore #87.

47. Tight end from Texas (2008-2013) who was a 3rd round pick and played only with the Packers. He caught 233 passes for 2,785 yards with 20 touchdown receptions and is a 2011 Super Bowl Champion. A bruised spinal cord encouraged him to retire at age 26. He wore #88.

49. The second half of the hyphenated surname of a defensive back from Alabama (2014-2018) who was a 1st round pick by the Packers and a 2016 Pro Bowler. He had 14 interceptions for Green Bay before moving onto Washington for 2018 and Chicago for 2019. He wore #21.

51. Defensive back from Bethune-Cookman (2005-2011) who was a 2nd round pick and a 3-time Pro Bowler for Green Bay. He is a 2011 Super Bowl Champion who played only for the Packers and he is a member of the Packer Hall of Fame. He had 21 career interceptions, with a league-leading 7 in 2008. He wore #36.

52. Receiver from Western Michigan (2006-2012) who was a 2nd round pick by the Packers, a 2-time Pro Bowler and a 2011 Super Bowl Champion. He had 3 years for the Packers with 1,100+ receiving yards and his 53 scoring catches are 6th most in Packer history. He went on to have two solid years with the Vikings. He wore #85.

54. Packer head coach (1988-1991) who compiled a 24-40 record in Green Bay with one winning season (10-6 in1989). He was allowed to lead the Colts (1996-1997) and went 12-20 for them. He had previously built a reputation as offensive coordinator with the Bengals (1981-1982) & Browns (1986-1987).

57. Defensive end/tackle from Boston College (2009-2015) who was a 1st round pick (taken 9th overall) and played only for the Packers. He was a 2011 Pro Bowler and is a 2011 Super Bowl Champion. He missed all of 2014 due to a torn biceps but did start every game in 3 of his 7 seasons. He wore #90.

58. Linebacker from Ohio State (2006-2014) who was a 1st round pick and taken 5th overall by the Packers. He was a huge college star, winning both the Jack Lambert Trophy and the Lombardi Award. He never made a Pro Bowl but is a 2011 Super Bowl Champion. He started every game in 5 seasons. He wore #50.

59. Aaron Rodgers played college football at
_____.

GREEN BAY PACKERS

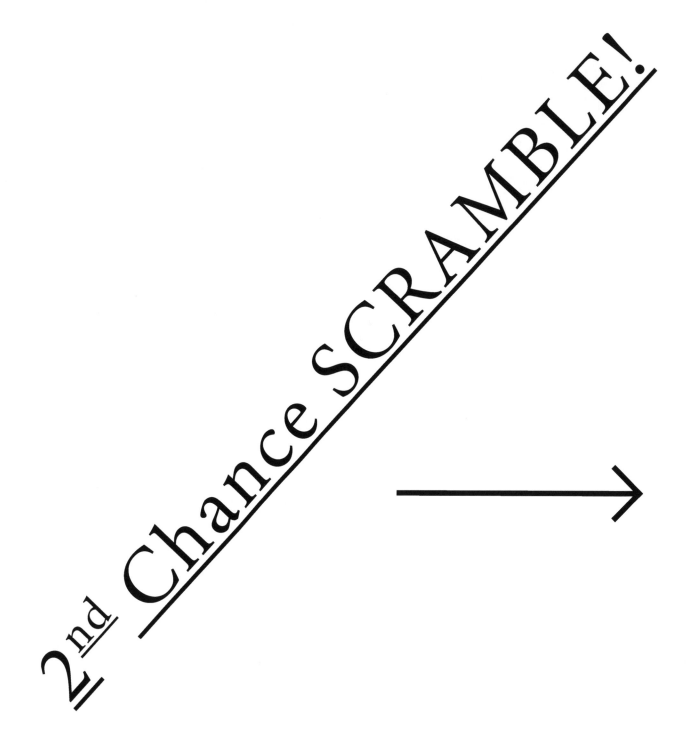

2ⁿᵈ Chance SCRAMBLE!

GREEN BAY PACKERS

ACROSS

1. CYCRAHMT   _ _ _ _ _ _ _ _
4. EETBNNT   _ _ _ _ _ _ _
8. KNHU   _ _ _ _
9. AHMRCU   _ _ _ _ _ _
11. IRDVRE   _ _ _ _ _ _
12. YEHD   _ _ _ _
13. AAHH   _ _ _ _
14. RSERHPA   _ _ _ _ _ _ _
15. REYPR   _ _ _ _ _
16. AESRPH   _ _ _ _ _ _
21. RTBEUL   _ _ _ _ _ _
22. EEPRPSP   _ _ _ _ _ _ _
24. ATTALAN   _ _ _ _ _ _ _
26. CHCOI   _ _ _ _ _
28. ORNBW   _ _ _ _ _
31. RASKFN   _ _ _ _ _ _
32. DHARWO   _ _ _ _ _ _
34. NKAPMMA   _ _ _ _ _ _ _
36. NOSEJ   _ _ _ _ _
38. BYRCOS   _ _ _ _ _ _
40. SIIWLMLA   _ _ _ _ _ _ _ _
42. LTINFOC   _ _ _ _ _ _ _
43. AESJM   _ _ _ _ _
44. SRICH   _ _ _ _ _
48. NOLDAD   _ _ _ _ _ _
50. KCJAE   _ _ _ _ _
53. GLELWNLO   _ _ _ _ _ _ _ _
55. AYCL   _ _ _ _
56. MHENSRA   _ _ _ _ _ _ _
60. ATRGN   _ _ _ _ _
61. ARYN   _ _ _ _
62. EDIDE   _ _ _ _ _
63. WIHET   _ _ _ _ _

DOWN

1. STHAWMET   _ _ _ _ _ _ _ _
2. NULHEYD   _ _ _ _ _ _ _
3. RNEMAEF   _ _ _ _ _ _ _
4. UKYLECB   _ _ _ _ _ _ _
5. HNGORLME   _ _ _ _ _ _ _ _
6. VEIRAR   _ _ _ _ _ _
10. AMDSA   _ _ _ _ _
15. PUAP   _ _ _ _
17. RSHARI   _ _ _ _ _ _
18. NLEVES   _ _ _ _ _ _
19. ANORA   _ _ _ _ _
20. SAM   _ _ _
21. NRTBATE   _ _ _ _ _ _ _
23. ITOTSN   _ _ _ _ _ _
25. ENOSJ   _ _ _ _ _
27. CBOB   _ _ _ _
28. KOBSOR   _ _ _ _ _ _
29. ASSRTK   _ _ _ _ _ _
30. ENRGE   _ _ _ _ _
33. SDONWOO   _ _ _ _ _ _ _
35. REMNZTAI   _ _ _ _ _ _ _ _
36. UILSJU   _ _ _ _ _ _
37. SSMI   _ _ _ _
39. ABLUGA   _ _ _ _ _ _
41. OWIKJASKM   _ _ _ _ _ _ _ _ _
45. SDEHLIS   _ _ _ _ _ _ _
46. LSENON   _ _ _ _ _ _
47. EFYLNI   _ _ _ _ _ _
49. DXI   _ _ _
51. ILLCOSN   _ _ _ _ _ _ _
52. NEJSNGIN   _ _ _ _ _ _ _ _
54. INFATNE   _ _ _ _ _ _ _
57. RIAJ   _ _ _ _
58. KAWH   _ _ _ _
59. LCA   _ _ _

CHICAGO BEARS

ACROSS

1. Wide-out from Central Florida (2012-2014 who came to the Bears after having been a 3- time Pro Bowler with the Broncos and Dolphins. He was a 2-time Pro Bowler with Chicago, catching 118 passes in 2012 and 100 passes in 2013. He then had one more Pro Bowl season with the Jets in 2015. He wore #15.

3. Kicker from Georgia (1985-1995) who was a 4th round pick by the Bears and a 1986 Super Bowl Champion. His 243 career field goals are the most in team history. His son, Drew, grew up to punt for Pittsburgh (2012) and Arizona (2014-2016). He wore #4.

6. The first name of the player referred to in 33 ACROSS.

9. Running back from Florida (1986-1993) who was a 1st round pick and only played for the Bears, for whom he was a 4-time Pro Bowler. He had 3 straight seasons with 1,000+ rushing yards (1988-1990) and his 6,166 career rushing yards are #3 all-time for the Bears. He is also #2 in career rushing touchdowns with 51. He wore #35.

11. The first name of the player referred to in 11 ACROSS.

13. The first name of the coach referred to in 30 DOWN.

16. Hall of Fame linebacker from Baylor (1981-1992) who was a 2nd round pick, only played for the Bears and was a 10-time Pro Bowler. He was a 1986 Super Bowl Champion and a 2-time NFL Defensive Player of the Year (1985 & 1988). His tenure as head coach of the 49ers (2009-2010), however, was not successful. He wore #50.

18. Wide-out/kick returner from Abilene Christian (2009-2011) who was a 5th round pick and only played for the Bears. He had a 102-yard kickoff return in 2009 and 900 receiving yards in 2010. He suffered a career-ending spinal cord injury in Dec. 2011, however, and he still walks with a limp. He wore #13.

19. Brash, lefty QB from UCLA (1999-2000) who was a 1st round pick. Injuries to veteran quarterbacks forced him to play before he was ready and he went just 3-12 as a starter. He was a better runner than passer (like another lefty, Bobby Douglass) and he never played another down after leaving the Bears at age 24. He wore #8.

20. Wide-out from Penn State (2018-2021) who had been a 2nd round pick by the Jaguars (2014-2017), for whom he was a 2015 Pro Bowler when he tied for the NFL lead with 14 touchdown catches. With the Bears he had 98 catches for 1,100 years in 2019 and 102 catches for 1,200 yards in 2020. In 2021, however, he was hurt and missed 7 games. He wears #12.

24. Kicker from Washington (1996-1999) who had earlier kicked for the Raiders (1985-1995), for whom he was a 1991 Pro Bowler and the 1993 leader with 35 field goals. For the Bears, his 76% success rate on field goals (63 for 83) is #2 all-time for those kickers with 80+ attempts. He wore #1.

25. Quarterback from TCU (2021) who had been a 2nd round pick by the Bengals (2011-2019), for whom he was a 3-time Pro Bowler. He went to Dallas for 2020 and ended up making 9 starts when Oak Prescott was hurt, winning 4 of them. He came to Chicago and started 2 games in 2021 before being benched for a younger player. He wears #14.

26. The first name of the player referred to in 7 DOWN.

27. Chicago head coach (2018-2021) who achieved a reputation as a creative coach as offensive coordinator for Kansas City (2017). His first Bears team went 12-4 and Chicago won the NFC Central for the first time since 2010. He has failed to break .500 since then, however.

29. Defensive back from Virginia Tech (2014-2020) who was a 1st round pick by the Bears and a 2-time Pro Bowler (2018-2019). In 2018, he tied for the NFL lead with 7 interceptions. He missed all of 2017 due to injury but appeared in all 96 games in his other 6 years with the Bears, starting

94 of them. He moved on to Denver in 2021. He wore #23.

31. The first name of the coach referred to in 3 DOWN.

32. The first name of the player referred to in 3 ACROSS.

35. Kicker from Michigan State (2000-2004) who was a 6th round pick. His 110 career field goals are #4 all-time for the Bears (with a 75% success rate) and he made all of his 133 extra point tries. He finished his career in 2005 with Minnesota. He wore #2.

36. Quarterback from Purdue (2005-2008) who was a 4th round pick by the Bears. He went 21-12 as a starter for Chicago before moving on to Denver (2009-2011), for whom he went 12-21 as a starter. He finished by going 9-7 as a starter with the Chiefs, Cowboys and Bills over 2011-2014. He wore #18.

37. Running back from Michigan (2001-2004) who was a 2nd round pick and the NFL Offensive Rookie of the Year when he had 1,183 rushing yards. He ran for 1,024 yards in 2003 before injuries piled up on him. His nickname was "A Train". He wore #35.

38. Defensive back from Alabama (2017-2021) who was a 4th round pick and has only played for the Bears to date. He was a Pro Bowler in 2018 when he had 6 interceptions, with 2 returned for touchdowns. He was also a 2019 Pro Bowler. So far he has not missed a game and has started all but 2 as of Nov 2021. He wears #39.

41. Kick returner/wide-out from Miami (2006-2013) who was a 2nd round pick by the Bears, a 3-time Pro Bowler and is a member of the NFL 2000s All-Decade Team. He returned the opening kick-off of the 2007 Super Bowl for a touchdown and he holds the NFL record with 20 regular season scores on kick returns. He wore #23.

42. Quarterback from Ohio State (2021) who was a 1st round pick. He has made just 7 starts as of November 2021 and, after a rocky start, has come on lately. It is hoped that the Bears have, at last, acquired that elusive "franchise quarterback". He wears #1.

44. Defensive back from Nebraska (2000-2008) who was a 2nd round pick by the Bears, a 2005 Pro Bowler and a 2007 Super Bowler. He is the only NFL player to end consecutive games with scoring interception returns. He was smart, a big hitter and was named one of "The 50 Greatest Bears". He wore #30.

45. Defensive end from North Carolina (2010-2013) who had been a 1st round pick by Carolina. He was a 3-time Pro Bowler with the Bears, while starting every game in his 4 seasons. He made a total of 9 Pro Bowls and he is a member of the NFL 2000s All-Decade Team. He had 160 career sacks and was also agile enough to play basketball for Carolina. He wore #90.

47. Kicker from Penn State (2002-2015) who, though undrafted, is #1 on the all-time Chicago list with 276 field goals. He was a 2006 Pro Bowler who helped the Bears reach the 2007 Super Bowl. With the 49ers (2017-2021) he has kicked another 119 field goals, with an 88% success rate. He wore #9.

49. The first name of the player referred to in 21 ACROSS.

50. Hall of Fame defensive end from Tennessee State (1983-1993) who was just an 8th round pick by the Bears. He was a 4-time Pro Bowler and a 1986 Super Bowl Champion. His 124.5 sacks are the most in team history. He went on to be a Super Bowl Champion again with the 1994 49ers (the year they destroyed the Chargers). He wore #95.

52. Quarterback from USC (2016) who had been a 4th round pick by the Eagles. He was brilliant in his first 3 years at USC but a poor senior season caused his draft position to slide. He threw just 50 passes for Philadelphia and then went 1-5 as a starter for a bad Bear team. He went on to appear in 8 games as a back-up in Buffalo (2018-2020). He wore #12.

54. The first name of the Chicago head coach (1993-1998) whose teams went just 40-56. His best teams went 9-7, in both 1994 and 1995, with a surprise Wild Card win at Minnesota in 1995. He went on to more success as the head man in Miami (2000-2004) with seasons of 11-5, 11-5 and 10-6. He had earlier won a ring as the Dallas DC (1992).

57. Defensive back from USC (1990-1996) who was a 1st round pick by the Bears. He was the NFL Defensive Rookie of the Year when he had a league-best, 10 interceptions and was a 3-time Pro Bowler for Chicago. He finished up with the Lions (1997-1999) and Redskins (2000). He wore #20.

58. The first name of the player referred to in 34 ACROSS.

59. Wide-out from USC (1993-1999) who was a 1st round pick by the Bears, for whom he had 2 years with 1,000+ receiving yards (1995-1996). He went on to have one more 1,000-yard season with the Chargers in 2001. He is tied for 4th all-time for the Bears with 329 catches. He wore #80.

61. Quarterback from Michigan (1987-1993) who was a 1st round pick by the Bears. He went 35-30 as a starter in Chicago and was a favorite whipping boy of his snarling head coach. He went on to play for the Colts, Ravens and Chargers before launching a successful college and NFL coaching career. He wore #4.

62. Wide-out from Fresno State (2004-2007) who was a 3rd round pick by the Bears and a member of the 2006 team that reached the Super Bowl. In 2007, he had his best year as a Bear with 951 receiving yards. With the Vikings in 2008, he scored on a 99-yard pass play against Chicago. He wore #80.

63. The first name of the player referred to in 30 ACROSS.

64. The first name of the player referred to in 7 ACROSS.

DOWN

1. Running back from Iowa State (2019-2021) who was a 3rd round pick by the Bears. He had 889 rushing yards as a rookie and 1,070 yards in 2020, but at the mid-point of 2021, he has missed 4 out of 9 games. He wears #32.

2. Brazilian-born kicker from Tulane (2017 & 2021-2021) who first played for the Chiefs (2014-2017). At the mid-point of the 2021 season, he has made 44 of his career field goal tries for the Bears (92%). Let's hope he can continue at this pace! He wears #2.

4. Defensive back from Louisiana-Lafayette (2003-2014) who was a 2nd round pick by the Bears and a 2-time Pro Bowler. He helped Chicago reach the 2007 Super Bowl and his 36 career interceptions are #3 in franchise history. He had an amazing knack for causing fumbles and no Bear has matched his 9 defensive touchdowns. He wore #33.

5. The first name of the player referred to in 8 DOWN.

7. Bear head coach (2013 2014) whose teams went just 8-8 and 5-11. He had previously served as offensive coordinator for the Browns, 49ers, Cardinals and Raiders and had a reputation for devising creative plays and was regarded as something of a "quarterback whisperer". He also led Montreal to Grey Cup Championships in 2009 and 2010.

8. Long-time NFL head coach who finished his career as the head man in Chicago (2015-2017). Sadly, his teams went just 6-10, 3-13 and 5-11. He had earlier guided the Panthers (2002-2010) to the 2004 Super Bowl and later, as Denver head coach (2011-2014), he led the Broncos to the 2014 Super Bowl.

10. Running back from Penn State (1998-2000) who was a 1st round pick by the Bears. He had 916 yards for a bad Bear team in 1999 but his career was marked by injuries and just plain poor play. He was out of the NFL at age 24. He wore #39 and #44.

12. The first name of the player referred to in 21 DOWN.

14. Quarterback from North Carolina State (1994-1998) who began with the Lions (1991-1993). With the Bears, he went just 18-28 as a starter but did manage to lead the team to that Wild Card win over the Vikings. He is #4 on the all-time Bear list with 913 completions. He wore #12.

15. Punter from Ball State (2001-2010) who came to the Bears from the Giants (1997-2000), for whom he set a Super Bowl record with 11 punts in a 34-7 thrashing by the Ravens. He helped the Bears reach the 2007 Super Bowl and his 878 punts are the 2nd most in Chicago history. He wore #4.

17. 5'6", 180-pound running back/returner from North Carolina A&T (2017-2021) who was a 4th round pick and a 2018 Pro Bowler when he had 1,600 all-purpose yards. He managed just 600 yards in 2019, however. He signed a 3-year deal in 2020 but tore an ACL in Game 3 and has been unable to play since then. He wears #29.

21. Tight end from Texas A&M (2013-2015) who had earlier been a 2nd round pick by Dallas (2008-2011). He was a 2014 Pro Bowler with the Bears when he had 90 catches but his exit from Chicago was bitter. He went on to be a 2017 Super Bowl Champion with the Patriots, starring in their stunning comeback win over Atlanta. He wore #83.

22. Quarterback from Vanderbilt (2009-2016) who came to the Bears after being a 1st round pick by Denver. He is Chicago's all-time leader in completions, passing yardage and in touchdown passes but his record as a starter was just 51-51. His pouty and seemingly disinterested demeanor did not go over well with the fan base. He wore #6.

23. The first name of the player referred to in 18 ACROSS.

26. Wide-out from Louisiana-Monroe (1999-2003 and 2008) who was a 3rd round pick by the Bears and a 2002 Pro Bowler. He had 100 catches in 2001 and had 2 seasons with 1,000+ receiving yards (2001 and 2002). He is tied for 4th all-time for the Bears with 329 career catches. He wore #86.

28. Quarterback from Florida (2003-2008) who was a Heisman runner-up and a 1st round pick by the Bears. He was often injured but, in his only full season, he led Chicago to a 13-3 record and a Super Bowl appearance vs. the Colts in 2007. He finished up with Washington (2010-2011), for whom he made 16 starts. He wore #8.

29. Quarterback from Michigan State and Arizona (2020) who had been a 3rd round pick by the Eagles (2012-2014 and 2017-2018). He came back to the Eagles to serve as a back-up to Carson Wentz, but led the team on a remarkable play-off run and Super Bowl Championship. With the Bears, however, there was no magic, as he went just 2-5 as a starter. He wore #9.

30. Undrafted center from Iowa (1981-1991) who was a 7-time Pro Bowler with the Bears and a 1986 Super Bowl Champion. He started every game in 7 of his 11 seasons in Chicago and is now a radio analyst on Bear broadcasts. He wore #63.

33. The first name of the player referred to in 13 DOWN.

34. Running back from Tulane (2008-2015) who was a 2nd round pick by the Bears and a 2-time Pro Bowler. He had 5 years for the Bears with 1,000+ rushing yards and 6 years with 50+ catches. In franchise history, only Walter Payton has more rushing yards and catches. He finished with the Jets (2016-2017). He wore #22.

37. Quarterback from North Carolina (2017-2020) who was a 1st round pick by the Bears. After an uneven rookie year, he led the Bears to a division title in 2018 but regressed in 2019. His numbers were better in 2920 but the front office decided he doesn't have what it takes to be "the guy". He is now a back-up in Buffalo. He wore #10.

38. Wide-out from South Carolina (2012-2016) who was a 2nd round pick by the Bears and a 2013 Pro Bowler when he had 1,133 receiving yards on 89 catches. In 2014 he had similar numbers but then signed on with the Eagles (2017-2020), for whom he became a Super Bowl Champion in 2018. He is #3 all-time for the Bears with 4,549 receiving yards. He wore #17.

39. The first name of the player referred to in 29 DOWN.

40. The first name of the player referred to in 9 ACROSS.

41. Running back from Indiana (2016-2018) who was a 5th round pick by the Bears and a surprise Pro Bowler as a rookie when he ran for 1,313 yards. In 2017 and 2018 his numbers declined only lightly. He moved on to the Eagles (2019-2021) for whom he has been a backup. He wore #24.

43. Offensive lineman from Oregon (2013-201) who was a 1st round pick by the Bears and has only played for Chicago to date. He was a 3-time Pro Bowler (2013-2015) but over his last 4 seasons, missed more than half of the team's games due to injury. He is the son of an NFL Hall of Famer. He wore #75.

46. Hall of Fame, Chicago head coach (1982-1992) who led the 1985 team to a dominating season and a Super Bowl Championship. He had been a 1st round pick by the Bears (1961-1966) for whom he helped revolutionize the tight end position. He wore #89.

48. Hall of Fame linebacker from New Mexico (2000-2012) who was a 1st round pick and an 8-time Pro Bowler. He only played for the Bears and was the 2005 NFL Defensive Player of the Year. He is a member of the NFL 200s All-Decade Team and he helped the Bears reach the 2007 Super Bowl. He wore #54.

51. Chicago head coach (2004-2012) who led the team to the 2007 Super Bowl. His career record with the Bears was 81-63 but he went on to go just 2-14 and 6-10 as the head man in Tampa (2014-2015). Next he tried to resurrect the sad program at Illinois (2016-2020) but never had a winning season.

52. Linebacker from Arizona (2003-2014) who was a 3rd round pick and a 7-time Pro Bowler. He only played for the Bears and helped the team reach the 2007 Super Bowl. He recorded 1,100 tackles, 19 forced fumbles, 16 interceptions and 15 sacks. He wore #55.

53. The first name of the player referred to in 33 DOWN.

55. Defensive back from Texas (2004-2009) who was a 4th round pick by the Bears, a 2005 Pro Bowler and a starter on the 2006 team that reached the Super Bowl. He had 19 interceptions for Chicago, with 2 scoring runbacks. He wore #31.

56. Chicago head coach (1999-2003) who posted a 35-45 record and had just one winning season. His 2001 team went 13-3 but lost its first playoff game to the Eagles. As the Buffalo head coach (2006-2009) he never had a winning season. He was a Yale grad and a Pro Bowl defensive back with the Lions and Bengals (1973-1980).

60. Linebacker from Buffalo (2018-2021) who had been a 1st round pick by the Raiders (2014-2017), for whom he was a 3-time Pro Bowler. He came to the Bears in a trade for which Jon Gruden was roundly criticized. To date, he has made 3 Pro Bowls. He wears #52.

CHICAGO BEARS

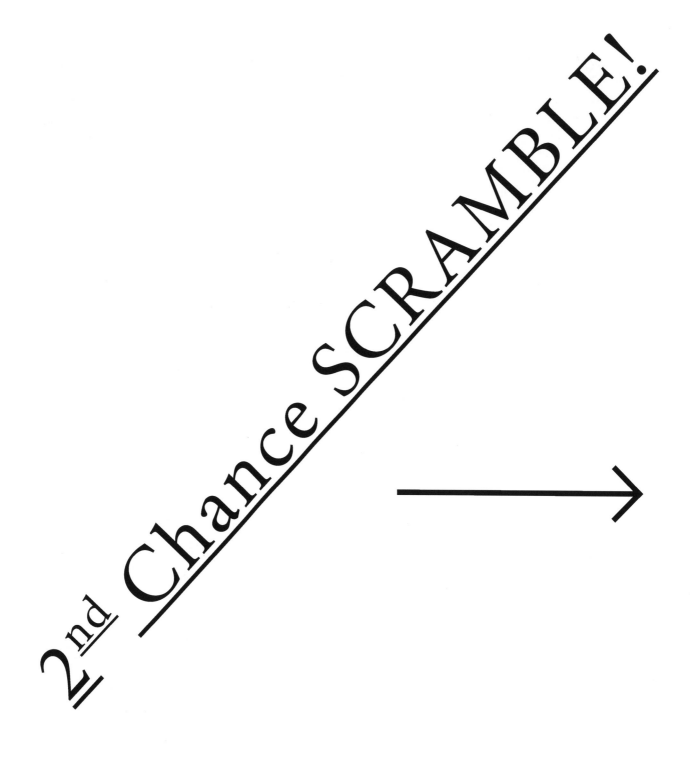

CHICAGO BEARS

ACROSS

1. LMSLAARH _ _ _ _ _ _ _ _
3. RTULEB _ _ _ _ _ _
6. CTURSI _ _ _ _ _ _
9. DENORNSA _ _ _ _ _ _ _ _
11. NALEL _ _ _ _ _
13. IDCK _ _ _ _
16. YNLESITGRA _ _ _ _ _ _ _ _ _ _
18. NOXK _ _ _ _
19. WCNNOM _ _ _ _ _ _
20. NNIOBOSR _ _ _ _ _ _ _ _
24. AJEERG _ _ _ _ _ _
25. NTDOAL _ _ _ _ _ _
26. BRDA _ _ _ _
27. ANYG _ _ _ _
29. LUEFLR _ _ _ _ _ _
31. JHON _ _ _ _
32. NKIVE _ _ _ _ _
35. REIENDG _ _ _ _ _ _ _
36. RNOOT _ _ _ _ _
37. HSMTAO _ _ _ _ _ _
38. ASNCJKO _ _ _ _ _ _ _
41. ERTSEH _ _ _ _ _ _
42. EDSLFI _ _ _ _ _ _
44. ONWBR _ _ _ _ _
45. PESRPEP _ _ _ _ _ _ _
47. ULGOD _ _ _ _ _
49. KLYE _ _ _ _
50. NTDE _ _ _ _
52. KREABLY _ _ _ _ _ _ _
54. DAEV _ _ _ _
57. ARCRREI _ _ _ _ _ _ _
58. IJM _ _ _
59. ONWAYC _ _ _ _ _ _
61. RUBAHAGH _ _ _ _ _ _ _ _
62. INERBAR _ _ _ _ _ _ _
63. RAKM _ _ _ _
64. EMIK _ _ _ _

DOWN

1. MNERGTOMOY _ _ _ _ _ _ _ _ _
2. OSNTAS _ _ _ _ _ _
4. ALLITNM _ _ _ _ _ _ _
5. KEIR _ _ _ _
7. ENTASMRT _ _ _ _ _ _ _ _
8. OXF _ _ _
10. ENSI _ _ _ _
12. ERX _ _ _
14. RMRAKE _ _ _ _ _ _
15. MNDARAY _ _ _ _ _ _ _
17. HCOEN _ _ _ _ _
21. TNBENET _ _ _ _ _ _ _
22. TRUCEL _ _ _ _ _ _
23. UPLA _ _ _ _
26. BEKORO _ _ _ _ _ _
28. MOSANRGS _ _ _ _ _ _ _ _
29. EFLOS _ _ _ _ _
30. GGRLNEEBHI _ _ _ _ _ _ _ _ _ _
33. NCIK _ _ _ _
34. ORTFE _ _ _ _ _
37. TKYIRBSU _ _ _ _ _ _ _ _
38. EERJFYF _ _ _ _ _ _ _
39. ELKY _ _ _ _
40. CDAE _ _ _ _
41. AHRWOD _ _ _ _ _ _
43. GLON _ _ _ _
46. ATIKD _ _ _ _ _
48. LHARURCE _ _ _ _ _ _ _ _
51. HISTM _ _ _ _ _
52. GIRBGS _ _ _ _ _ _
53. ATANHN _ _ _ _ _ _
55. HREAVS _ _ _ _ _ _
56. OUJARN _ _ _ _ _ _
60. CAKM _ _ _ _

ATLANTA FALCONS

ACROSS

1. Quarterback from Washington (1997-2001) who had been a 3rd round pick by the Colts (1988-1989). He finally came to Atlanta after playing for 4 more teams. He made his only 2 Pro Bowls with the Falcons and he led the 1998 team to a Super Bowl. He went 34-33 as a starter. He wore #12.

4. Linebacker from Georgia Tech (1998-2008) who was a 1st round pick by Atlanta and a 5-time Pro Bowler. He was a key player for the 1998 Super Bowl team as a rookie and he started every game in 8 straight seasons (2001-2008). He is #3 alltime for Atlanta with 888 solo tackles. He wore #56.

6. 5'10", 180-pound receiver from New Mexico (1994-2001) who had been a 6th round pick by the Jets (1990-1993). With Atlanta he had 4 seasons with 1,000+ receiving yards and he had 111 catches in his only Pro Bowl season (1994). He had 6 straight years with 60+ catches for Atlanta. He wore #81.

9. Linebacker from LSD (2016-2019) who was a 2nd round pick by the Falcons. As a rookie he returned 2 interceptions for touchdowns, including a 90-yarder vs. the Saints. In 2017 he was a Pro Bowler when he started every game. In the 2019 finale, he ended an overtime game vs. Tampa with an interception score. He wears #45.

11. Quarterback from Oregon (1987-1993) who was a 1st round pick by Atlanta and a 1991 Pro Bowler. He went 23-43 as a starter for the Falcons. He had at least 5 concussions in 14 months, which limited him to just 2 starts in 1993 and hastened his retirement. He is #3 all-time for Atlanta with 14,000 passing yards. He wore #12.

12. Defensive back from Louisville (1997-2003) who had been a 3rd round pick by the Colts (1993-1996). He was a 1998 Pro Bowler for Atlanta's 1st Super Bowl team and started every game in 5 straight seasons (1997-2001). His 30 interceptions are #3 all-time for the Falcons. He wore #34.

15. Receiver from Northern Arizona (1988-1993) who was a 7th round pick by Atlanta. His career-year was 1991 when he had 1,122 receiving yards on only 50 catches, leading the NFL with an average of 22 yards per reception. He is #7 all-time for the Falcons with 4,220 receiving yards. He wore #81.

16. The first name of the player referred to in 9 ACROSS.

20. Running back from North Texas (1991-1994) who was a 6th round pick by the Falcons and had a career-best 1,185 rushing yards in 1993. He went on to help the Steelers reach the 1996 Super Bowl by leading the team in rushing yards. He wore #41 & #33.

22. Atlanta head coach (2004-2006) whose teams went 11-5, 8-8 and 7-9. Later, with Seattle (2009) he had a 5-11 season. He then went to UCLA (2012-2017) where his teams went 46-30. His dad was the head coach for both the Saints and Colts and is famous for launching a post-game rant about "Playoffs !!!???"

23. Undrafted linebacker from Valdosta State (1987-2000) who was a 5-time Pro Bowler and only played for Atlanta. He made 189 starts, including every game for the 1998 Super Bowl team. He is #1 all-time for Atlanta in solo tackles (1,639!). He is a member of the Falcons Ring of Honor and the team has retired his #58.

24. Undrafted offensive tackle from Wake Forest (2005-2012) who was a 2010 Pro Bowler and made 101 starts for Atlanta, including every game in 5 straight seasons (2008-2012). He finished up with 15 starts for the 2013 Dolphins. He wore #77.

25. Center from Cal (2016-2019) who had been a 1st round pick by the Browns (2009-2015), for whom he made 3 Pro Bowls. He has also been a 3-time Pro Bowler for Atlanta and has started all 64 Falcon games since joining the team. He wears #51.

28. The first name of the player referred to in 2 DOWN.

32. Receiver from UAB (2005-2015) who was 1st round pick and only played for Atlanta. He made 4 Pro Bowls and led the NFL with 115 catches

in 2010. He had 6 straight years with 1,100+ receiving yards and is #1 all-time for Atlanta with 63 scoring catches. He is a member of the Falcons Ring of Honor. He wore #84.

33. Running back from Florida State (2014-2019) who was a 4th round pick and has only played for Atlanta to date. He made 2 Pro Bowls when he had seasons with 1,000+ rushing yards (2015 and 2016). He helped the 2016 team reach the Super Bowl and he is #6 all-time for Atlanta with 3,972 rushing yards. He wears #24.

36. The first name of the player referred to in 22 ACROSS.

27. Left-footed, Danish-born kicker from Michigan State (1995-2000 & 2006-2007) who had been a 4th round pick by the Saints (1982-1994). He was a 1995 Pro Bowler with Atlanta and went on to propel the 1998 team to the Super Bowl with an overtime field goal in the NFL Championship Game. He wore #5.

38. The first name of the coach referred to in 27 DOWN.

39. The first name of the player referred to in 6 ACROSS.

40. Tight end from Stanford (2016-2019) who was 3rd round pick by Atlanta and a 2-time Pro Bowler (2018 & 2019). He had 2 years with 70+ catches and 650+ receiving yards for the Falcons before signing a 4-year deal with the Browns in 2020. He wore #81.

42. The first name of the player referred to in 26 DOWN.

43. 5'10", 185-pound receiver from Rice (1994-1997) who was a 2nd round pick by Atlanta and made the switch from college option-quarterback. He had one year for the Falcons with 1,000 receiving yards and 2 more with 900+ yards. He finished up with one more productive season with the 1998 Bucs. He wore #87.

44. Since 2002, the Falcons have been owned by Arthur _____.

47. Defensive end from Tennessee (1992-1999) who was a 2nd round pick and a 1997 Pro Bowler for Atlanta. He made 87 starts for the Falcons, including every game for the 1998 Super Bowl team. He had 3 seasons for the Falcons with 10+ sacks and his 58.5 career sacks are #2 all-time for Atlanta. He wore #90.

49. Receiver from Alabama (2011-2019) who was taken 6th overall by Atlanta and has only played for the Falcons. He has made 7 Pro Bowls to date and has led the NFL once in catches (2015) and twice in receiving yards (2015 & 2018). He has also had 6 straight years with 1,300+ receiving yards. He wears #11.

52. The first name of the player referred to in 9 DOWN.

54. The first name of the player referred to in 25 DOWN.

56. Colorful Atlanta head coach (1990-1993) who had a 10-6 season in 1991 but finished with an overall mark of just 27-37. He had earlier been the head coach of the Houston Oilers (1985-1989) where his teams went 33-32. Among other things, he said "The NFL stands for Not For Long."

61. Receiver from Rutgers (2016-2019) who had been a 3rd round pick by the Bengals (2012-2015). With Atlanta, he had 3 seasons with 60+ catches and 650+ receiving yards. He was traded to the Patriots in October 2019. He wore #12.

62. The Falcons have a woeful 2-14 all-time record against the _____, their worst showing against any opponent.

63. Defensive back from Missouri (2009-2015) who was a 2nd round pick by Atlanta and a 2012 Pro Bowler. He only played for the Falcons and made 72 starts with 16 career interceptions. He wore #25.

64. The first name of the player referred to in 5 DOWN.

65. On their way to the 2017 Super Bowl, the Falcons blasted the _____ 44-21, in the NFC Championship Game.

DOWN

1. Running back from Indiana (2015-2018) who was a 3rd round pick by Atlanta. He helped the 2016 team reach the Super Bowl and had a career-high 800 rushing yards in 2018. In 2019 he had 500 rushing yards for the 49er team that also reached the Super Bowl. He wore #26.

2. Quarterback from Boston College (2008-2019) who was taken 3rct overall by Atlanta. He has made 4 Pro Bowls to date and has only played for the Falcons. He was the NFL MVP in 2016, the year he led the team to the Super Bowl. He wears #2.

3. Receiver from Michigan State (1990-1994) who had been a 1st round pick by the Colts (1989). He was a 4-time Pro Bowler for Atlanta and he led the NFL with 15 scoring catches in 1993. He had 4 seasons with 1,000+ receiving yards for the Falcons and one more for the 1997 Chiefs. His rapper girl-friend burned down his house in 1996. His 56 scoring catches are #4 all-time for Atlanta. He wore #80.

4. Undrafted kicker from Baylor (2009-2019) who had earlier played for the Giants (2002-2003) and Buccaneers (2005-2008). He made his only Pro Bowl for the 2016 Super Bowl team and he has had 5 seasons with 30+ field goals for Atlanta. His 259 career field goals are #1 all-time for the Falcons. He wears #3.

5. Undrafted kicker from Michigan (2001-2004) who came to Atlanta after 2 years in the Arena League. In 2002 he led the NFL with 32 field goals and his 98 field goals with Atlanta are #5 all-time for the Falcons. He also had 58 field goals for the Giants, 54 for the Jets and 98 for the Cardinals. He wore #4.

7. Quarterback from Northwestern State (Louisiana) (1993-1996) who came to Atlanta after 3 years in the USFL and 8 years with the Saints (1985-1992). For the Falcons (1993-1996) he had his only Pro Bowl season in 1993 but went just 7-18 as a starter. His 7,053 passing yards are 8th all-time for Atlanta. He wore #3.

8. Defensive back from Oklahoma (1984-1994) who was a 2nd round pick by Atlanta, for whom he was a 1988 Pro Bowler when he led the NFL with 10 interceptions. His 30 career interceptions are #3 all-time for the Falcons. He went on to become a Super Bowl Champ with the 1995 Cowboys. He wore #25.

10. Hall of Fame defensive back from Florida State (1989-1993) who was taken 5th overall by Atlanta, for whom he was a 3-time Pro Bowler. He had 24 picks and 3 defensive touchdowns for the Falcons plus 5 touchdowns on kick returns. He went on to be a 2-time Super Bowl Champion with other teams. He wore #21.

13. Tight end from North Carolina (2001-2007) who was a 2nd round pick and 4- time Pro Bowler for Atlanta. He is #7 all-time for the Falcons in both catches (316) and touchdown catches (35). He has the ideal name for a punishing blocker who can run over people. He finished with the Titans (2008-2009). He wore #83.

14. Quarterback from Purdue and Illinois (1994-1996) who had been taken 1st overall by the Colts (1990-1993). He went 16-19 as a starter for Atlanta and 46-78 in his 12-year career that included stops in Oakland, Minnesota and Washington. He had immense talent but his odd personality was off-putting. He wore #1.

17. The 2017 Falcons were the last Atlanta team to win a playoff game to date with a 26-13 win over the _____ in the Wild Card round.

18. Defensive back from Florida (2016-2019) who was a 1st round pick by Atlanta and has only played for the Falcons to date. He started 14 games as a rookie and all 16 games in his Pro Bowl season of 2017. 2018 was ruined by an ACL tear in the season opener and 2019 was lost due to an Achilles tear in Week 3. He wears #22.

19. The first name of the player referred to in 19 ACROSS.

21. Hall of Fame tight end from Cal (2009-2013) who had been a 1st round pick by the Chiefs (1997-2008), for whom he was a 10-time Pro Bowler. He made 4 more Pro Bowls with Atlanta. He holds the NFL record for most catches all-time by a tight end (1,375) and most receiving yards (15,127). He wore #88.

22. Receiver/returner from Texas (1995-1996) who had been a 1st round pick by the Browns (1989-1994). With Atlanta he had 104 catches for 1,189 yards in 1995. He went on to play 6 more seasons for 5 teams and retired with 10 touchdowns on punt returns and 2 more on kickoffs. He wore #21.

23. The first name of the player referred to in 14 DOWN.

25. Receiver from Mesa State (Colorado) (1998-2001) who, as a Charger (1994-1997), helped San Diego reach the 1995 Super Bowl and then led the NFL with 14 scoring catches in 1996. With Atlanta he had 1,187 receiving yards in 1998 and then had another 1,000-yard-season in 1999 with Miami. He wore #80.

26. Defensive back from Washington (2013-2019) who was a 1st round pick by Atlanta, for whom he was a 2015 Pro Bowler. He started 97 games for the Falcons, including every game in 4 of his 7 seasons. He also helped the team reach the 2017 Super Bowl. He signed with the Lions for 2020. He wore #21.

27. Hall of Fame defensive end from Pitt (1994-1995) who had been taken 4th overall by the Vikings (1985-1993), for whom he was a 6-time Pro Bowler with 97 of his career 150.5 sacks. He was a 1995 Pro Bowler for Atlanta and then had 15 sacks at age 37 for the 1998 49ers. He died of brain cancer at age 58. He wore #56.

29. The first name of the player referred to in 2 ACROSS.

30. Electric, left-handed quarterback from Virginia Tech (2001-2008) who was taken 1st overall by Atlanta and a 3-time Pro Bowler. He went 38-28-1 as a starter for Atlanta and, after a "break", went on to another Pro Bowl with the Eagles (2010). His 6,100 career rushing yards are a record for NFL quarterbacks. He wore #7.

31. 5'10", 245-pound running back from Northern Illinois (2008-2012) who had been a 5th round pick by the Chargers (2004-2007). He was a 2-time Pro-Bowler for Atlanta and had 3 years with 1,300+ rushing yards, including 1,699 in 2008. He is #1 all-time for Atlanta with 60 rushing touchdowns. He wore #33.

34. Defensive end from South Carolina (2006-2012) who had been a 1st round pick by the Jets (2000-2005), for whom he was a 3-time Pro Bowler with 54 career sacks. With Atlanta he made another Pro Bowl and had 68.5 sacks, the most in franchise history. He went on to get 11.5 sacks for Arizona at age 35 in 2013. He wore #55.

35. Defensive back from Arkansas State (1987-1996) who was an 11th round pick and 4-time Pro Bowler who only played for Atlanta. He earned elite status as a special teams player. He wore #37.

39. Atlanta head coach (1997-2003) whose teams went just 49-59-1, but he did have a 14-2 record with the 1998 Super Bowl team. Earlier (1981-1992), his Denver teams went 110-73-1 and made it to 3 Super Bowls.

40. Defensive back from Virginia Tech (2004-2007) who was taken 8th overall by Atlanta, for whom he made 2 Pro Bowls and recorded 17 interceptions. He was also a Pro Bowler for the 2010 Redskins (2008-2017) when he tied an NFL record with a 4-interception game (all off of Jay Cutler). He wore #21.

41. Running back from Utah (1994-2001) who was a 7th round pick and only played for Atlanta. He was a 1998 Pro Bowler when he led the NFL with 1,846 rushing yards for Atlanta's 1st Super Bowl team. He had 4 years with 1,000+ rushing yards before a torn ACL in Week 3 of the 2001 season ended his career. He wore #32.

42. Undrafted kicker from UCLA (1991-1994) who had earlier played for Seattle (1982-1990). He was a 1993 Pro Bowler for Atlanta and his 84 field goals are #5 alltime for the Falcons. He went on to kick another 127 of his 366 career field goals with Pittsburgh (1995-1998). He wore #9.

45. The first name of the player referred to in 4 ACROSS.

46. Defensive end from Virginia (1999-2006) who was a 1st round pick and a 2006 Pro Bowler for Atlanta. He had 3 years with 10+ sacks for the Falcons and his 58 career sacks are #3 all-time for Atlanta. In 2007 he was the NFL Defensive Player of the Year for Seattle when he led the NFL with 14.5 sacks. He wore #97.

48. 5'11", 265-pound running back from Pitt (1994-1996) who had been a 1st round pick by the Saints (1988-1992). He made his only Pro Bowl with Atlanta in 1995 when he had his only 1,000-yard rushing season. He died of a brain tumor in Atlanta at age 39 in 2006. His nickname was "Iron Head". He wore #34.

49. The first name of the player referred to in 10 DOWN.

50. Atlanta head coach (2008-2014) whose teams went 66-46. He had 2 teams that went 13-3 and his 2012 team went to the NFC Championship Game. His 67 total wins are the most in franchise history. He went on to be the defensive coordinator for the Buccaneers (2016-2018).

51. Receiver from Louisville (2008-2014) who was a 3rd round pick by Atlanta. He had a career-year in 2013 when injuries to starters thrust him into the spotlight. He responded with 85 catches for 1,067 yards. He finished up with 3 years as a parttimer for the Titans (2015-2017).

53. The 1998 Atlanta team went to the Super Bowl after beating the _____ 30-27 in overtime in the NFL Championship Game.

55. Defensive back/returner from Notre Dame (2002-2006) who had been a 3rd round pick by the Eagles (1998-1999). He led the NFL in punt return yards in 2003 for Atlanta and was a 2004 Pro Bowler. In his 11-year NFL career, he had 8 touchdowns on kick returns and 15,000 total return yards. He wore #20.

57. Offensive tackle from Northwestern (1990-1993) who had been taken 4th overall by the Colts (1983-1989), for whom he was a 6-time Pro Bowler. He was a 1991 Pro Bowler for Atlanta and he missed just one game in his 4 seasons with the Falcons, starting every game in his last 3 seasons. He wore #71.

58. 5'9", 180-pound running back from Florida State (2002-2007) who had been a 1st round pick by Tampa (1997-2001), for whom he was a 2-time Pro Bowler. He made another Pro Bowl with Atlanta (2005) and had 3 straight years with 1,000+ rushing yards. He is a member of the Falcons Ring of Honor. He wore #28.

59. From 1992-2016 the Falcons played in the Georgia _____.

60 The first name of the coach referred to in 34 DOWN.

ATLANTA FALCONS

2nd Chance SCRAMBLE!

→

ATLANTA FALCONS

ACROSS

1. DAHERNCL   _ _ _ _ _ _ _ _
4. ROIOGNBK   _ _ _ _ _ _ _ _
6. SITHMA   _ _ _ _ _ _
9. JENSO   _ _ _ _ _
11. MIRELL   _ _ _ _ _ _
12. ANHCUBNA   _ _ _ _ _ _ _ _
15. NYHEAS   _ _ _ _ _ _
16. CIERR   _ _ _ _ _
20. PGAREM   _ _ _ _ _ _
22. RAOM   _ _ _ _
23. UGGTEL   _ _ _ _ _ _ _
24. AOBCL   _ _ _ _ _
25. MCAK   _ _ _ _
28. TATM   _ _ _ _
32. EITWH   _ _ _ _ _
33. FAERMNE   _ _ _ _ _ _ _
36. UCHCK   _ _ _ _ _
37. EENNSADR   _ _ _ _ _ _ _ _
38. DNA   _ _ _
39. AYR   _ _ _
40. EOOPHR   _ _ _ _ _ _
42. AJALM   _ _ _ _ _
43. NAULMEE   _ _ _ _ _ _ _
44. NAKLB   _ _ _ _ _
47. ISTHM   _ _ _ _ _
49. ENSOJ   _ _ _ _ _
52. FJEF   _ _ _ _
54. ONMR   _ _ _ _
56. NILEAVLLG   _ _ _ _ _ _ _ _ _
61. ASUN   _ _ _ _
62. LCSTO   _ _ _ _ _
63. OEOMR   _ _ _ _ _
64. NAEDR   _ _ _ _ _
65. EARPCSK   _ _ _ _ _ _ _

DOWN

1. MNOCALE   _ _ _ _ _ _ _
2. RANY   _ _ _ _
3. RNSOI   _ _ _ _ _
4. ABYNRT   _ _ _ _ _ _
5. EFYLE   _ _ _ _ _
7. RHEBET   _ _ _ _ _ _
8. CASE   _ _ _ _
10. NDASSER   _ _ _ _ _ _ _
13. ERULMRPC   _ _ _ _ _ _ _ _
14. ERGOG   _ _ _ _ _ _ _
17. RSMA   _ _ _ _
18. NELA   _ _ _ _
19. ELXA   _ _ _ _
21. ZOGZLNAE   _ _ _ _ _ _ _ _
22. MLEFTAC   _ _ _ _ _ _ _
23. TNOY   _ _ _ _
25. TARIMN   _ _ _ _ _ _
26. NRTFTAU   _ _ _ _ _ _ _
27. ONDMEAL   _ _ _ _ _ _ _
29. CRHIS   _ _ _ _ _
30. VKCI   _ _ _ _
31. RTRENU   _ _ _ _ _ _
34. ABAMRAH   _ _ _ _ _ _ _
35. EHLLYES   _ _ _ _ _ _ _
39. VRSEEE   _ _ _ _ _ _
40. LLAH   _ _ _ _
41. SODNRAEN   _ _ _ _ _ _ _ _
42. NJNHSOO   _ _ _ _ _ _ _
45. THEIK   _ _ _ _ _
46. YNEKER   _ _ _ _ _ _
48. HERWYDA   _ _ _ _ _ _ _
49. AYJ   _ _ _
50. HMSTI   _ _ _ _ _
51. GLSDOAU   _ _ _ _ _ _ _
53. GVNKSII   _ _ _ _ _ _ _
55. USOMSR   _ _ _ _ _ _
57. NNITOH   _ _ _ _ _ _
58. NUDN   _ _ _ _
59. MEDO   _ _ _ _
60. EIKM   _ _ _ _

CXXV

DETROIT LIONS

ACROSS

1. Linebacker from Ohio State (1988-1995) who was a 2nd round pick by Detroit and a 4-time Pro Bowler. He is the all-time franchise leader with 1,020 solo tackles. He finished with Buffalo (1996-1997) and since 2001, has been a steady presence as a color commentator on both college and NFL telecasts. He wore #54.

8. The first name of the coach referred to in 15 ACROSS.

9. Guard from Eastern Michigan (2017-2018) who had been a 4th round pick and a 2011 Super Bowl Champion for Green Bay. He was a 2017 Pro Bowler with Detroit but missed 10 games in 2018 due to injury and then retired. He wore #76.

11. Running back from Notre Dame (2013-2018) who was a 6th round pick by Detroit. He had just 1,000 career rushing yards but was extremely valuable as a pass receiver, catching 285 passes, with 80 coming in 2015. He was mainly used as a 3rd down back and so many of his catches resulted in first downs. He wore #25.

12. Defensive end from Ghana and SMU (2013-2018) who was taken 5th overall by Detroit and was 2015 Pro Bowler when he had 14.5 sacks. He had 12 sacks for the Lions in 2017 and then went on to Seattle (2019) and San Francisco (2020). He wore #94.

13. Detroit head coach (2014-2017) who went 11-5 in his first year and followed with seasonal marks of 7-9, 9-7 and 9-7. He is the first Lions head coach to have a winning career record since Joe Schmidt (1967-1972). He had earlier led the Colts (2009-2011) to the 2010 Super Bowl in his first season as a head coach.

15. Wide out from Virginia (1998-2002) who was a 2nd round pick and only played for Detroit. He had a career-year in 1999 with 81catches for 1,338 yards but injuries prevented him from reaching those numbers again. He has gone on to careers as a minister and high school football coach back where he grew up. He wore #82.

16. Detroit head coach (2018-2020) who had been a 3-time Super Bowl Champion as the New England defensive coordinator. He was a failure with the Lions, however, as his teams had a cumulative record of just 13-29-1. He was fired after 11 games in 2020. I never thought the backward hat was a good look.

19. Quarterback from USC (1989-1993) who was a 6th round pick by Detroit. He went 21-26 as a starter for the Lions with 49 interceptions against just 38 touchdown passes. He has gone on to make a number of cheesy weight-loss commercials for Lipozene with his actress/singer spouse. He wore #9.

20. Defensive back from Mississippi State (2013-2019) who was a 2nd round pick by Detroit and a 3-time Pro Bowler. He had 19 interceptions for the Lions and led the NFL in 2017 with 8 of them. In March 2020 he was dealt to the Eagles, for whom he has made 30 starts to date as well as a 2021 Pro Bowl berth. He wore #24.

23. Wide-out from Notre Dame (2014-2018) who had been a 2nd round pick and a 2014 Super Bowl Champion for Seattle. With Detroit he had 4 straight seasons with 90+ catches and two with 1,000+ receiving yards. He went on to spend 2018 with the Eagles and 2019-2020 with the Giants. He wore #15.

24. The 1991 Lions were the last Detroit team to win a post-season game, with a 38-6 thrashing of _____ in the Divisional Round.

25. The first name of the player referred to in 5 DOWN.

28. 5'9", 180-pound wide-out from Miami (1991-1996) who had been a 2nd round pick by New Orleans. With Detroit he had two big years, with 108 catches for 1,488 yards in 1995 and then 94 catches for 1,021 yards in 1996. His 428 career catches are the 4th most in franchise history. He wore #80.

29. Quarterback from Oregon (2002-2005) who was taken 3rd overall by Detroit. He was a mammoth bust, going just 18-37 as a starter with more interceptions than touchdown passes. He went

on to play poorly for Miami (2006) and Atlanta (2007) as well. He wore #3.

32. The first name of the player referred to in 62 DOWN.

35. Heisman-winning wide-out/returner from Michigan (1999-2002) who had been a 1st round pick by Washington (1992-1994). He was a 1997 Super Bowl Champion with Green Bay and was the game's MVP. With Detroit, he had 2 scores on punt returns but was never a polished receiver. That in-game Heisman pose at Michigan was a bit much. He wore #18 and #80.

36. Wide-out from Georgia Tech (2007-2015) who was taken 2nd overall by Detroit and only played for the Lions. He was a 6-time Pro Bowler and had 6 straight seasons with 1,000+ receiving yards (2010-2015). He retired at the peak of his game, citing health concerns and the team's lack of success. He holds all Lion career receiving records. He wore #81.

38. The first name of the coach referred to in 54 DOWN.

39. The first name of the coach referred to in 49 DOWN.

40. The first name of the player referred to in 60 DOWN.

41. Undrafted quarterback from Central Washington (2006-2008) who had earlier played for Seattle (1996-2000) and Cincinnati (20012-2005). With Detroit, he went 10-26 as a starter but in 2006 became just the 2nd Lion to reach 4,000 passing yards in a season. However, he led the NFL in 2007 in interceptions. He wore #8.

43. Left-handed quarterback from Utah (1994 1998) who had been a 4th round pick by Miami (1990-1993). He went 27-30 as a starter for Detroit but at least had more touchdown passes than interceptions (79/57). He was the first Detroit passer to reach 4,000 yards through the air in a season. He finished as a back-up for the Ravens (1999) and Bengals (2000). He wore #19.

45. Linebacker from Boston College (1995-2001) who was a 5th round pick and 2-time Pro Bowler for Detroit. He only played for the Lions and he led the team in tackles in 4 straight seasons (1997-2000). A back injury limited him to just 4 games in 2001 and he retired at age 29. He wore #57.

47. Detroit head coach (1997-2000) whose teams went 27-30, with a best record of 9-7 in 1997. He quit after 9 games in 2000 due to frustration with the organization and the team's unwillingness to "fight back". Me had earlier posted 47-33 mark with San Diego and guided the Chargers to the 1995 Super Bowl, where they were obliterated by the 49ers.

50. Wide-out from Cal (2016-2020) who had been a 5th round pick by Cincinnati (2012-2015). He had a career year for Detroit in 2017 with 1,101 receiving yards. He missed 7 games due to injury in 2018 but came back with 62 catches in 2019 and 76 in 2020. Evidently fond of losing, he signed a 2-year deal with Jacksonville and caught 73 balls in 2021. He wore #11.

52. The 1997 Lions were beaten by _____ in the Wild Card Round by a score of 20-10.

54. Nose tackle from Nebraska (2010-2014) who was taken 2nd overall by Detroit. He was a 4-time Pro Bowler for the Lions, despite earning a reputation as a dirty player. He moved on to the Dolphins (2015-2017), Rams (2018) and Buccaneers (2019-2021), for whom he became a Super Bowl Champion in 2021. He wore #90.

55. Tight end from New Mexico (1995-2001) who was a 3rd round pick by Detroit and a 1999 Pro Bowler when he had a career-best 47 catches. He caught 192 passes for the Lions but was better known for his blocking skills. He wore #86.

58. The first name of the player referred to in 61 ACROSS.

62. Undrafted, possession-receiver from Northern Iowa who led the NFL with 98 catches (for 1,086 yards) in 2006. He had another 61 catches in 2007 before concussion issues forced his retirement. He wore #87.

63. Center from Maryland (1985-1997) who was a 2nd round pick by Detroit and a 3-time Pro Bowler. He started 161 games for the Lions, including every game in 9 of his 13 seasons. The player referred to in 39 DOWN credited this man's blocking for much of his own amazing success. He wore #53.

64. The first name of the player referred to in 43 ACROSS.

65. 350-pound defensive tackle from Texas (2001-2007) who was a 1st round pick by Detroit and a 2-time Pro Bowler. Besides being a fierce run-stopper, he was agile enough to record 29 sacks for the Lions. He went on to play well for 6 more years with the Browns (2008-2010), Saints (2011) and Giants (2011-2013). He wore #92.

66. Cornerback from North Carolina (2003-2006) who had been a 2nd round pick by the Rams (1999-2002). He was a 2-time Pro Bowler for Detroit and recorded 19 of his 43 career interceptions with the Lions. He finished with the Broncos (2002-2008) and 49ers (2009). He wore #32.

DOWN

2. Undrafted kicker from Central Florida (2014-2020) who had been a 2014 Pro Bowler with Denver (2007-2014). He was a 2016 Pro Bowler for Detroit and his 179 field goals are #3 in team history. He moved on to Arizona in 2021. He wore #5.

3. Upper Peninsula native and Detroit head coach (2003-2005) whose first two teams went 5-11 and 6-10. He was fired in 2005 with the team at 4-7. He had earlier won 3 NFC West titles with the 49ers (1997-2002), losing to Green Bay in the 1997 NFC Championship Game.

4. Quarterback from Utah State (1980-1989) who was a 4th round pick and only played for Detroit. He went 28-29 as a starter with just 55 touchdown passes vs. 70 interceptions (yes, defensive backs could get away with A LOT more back then). The suicide of his teen aged son drove him to unravel but he recovered to become a speaker on the topic. He wore #17.

5. Wide-out from Texas (2004-2008) who was a 1st round pick by Detroit and a 2006 Pro Bowler when he led the NFL with 1,310 receiving yards. He went on to unspectacular seasons with Dallas (2009-2010) and Chicago (2011). For a guy taken 7th overall in the draft, he has to be regarded as a disappointment. He wore #11.

6. 330-pound nose tackle from SMU (1987-1992) who was a 3rd round pick by Detroit and a 3-time Pro Bowler. He was a virtually-immovable run-stopper, despite constant double-teaming. He went on to play well for 7 more seasons with Cleveland (1993), Oakland (1995-1996) and Minnesota (1997-1999). He wore #93.

7. Quarterback from Eastern Michigan (1998-2004) who was a 2nd round pick by Detroit. He went just 9-27 as a starter for the Lions but at least his touchdown pass/interception ratio wasn't that awful (61/52). He went on to a long tour as a back-up with Pittsburgh (202-2010). He wore #10.

10. Receiver from Northern Illinois (2017-2020) who was a 3rd round pick by Detroit and a 2019 Pro Bowler when he led the NFL with 11 touchdown catches. He had two years with 1,000+ receiving yards for the Lions (2018-2019) but missed 11 games due to injury in 2020. With the dysfunctional Giants in 2021, he had just 37 catches. He wore #19.

13. Running back from Tennessee (2000-2002) who had been a 1st round pick by Jacksonville (1995-1999). With Detroit, he had two years with 1,100+ rushing yards (2000 and 2002) and despite playing just 3 seasons for the Lions, is #10 on the team's all-time rushing yards list with 2,890. He wore #34.

14. The first name of the player referred to in 26 DOWN.

17. Tight end from Oklahoma State (200-2016) who was a 1st round pick and only played for Detroit. He had 71 catches in 2010, 83 in 2011 and 301 in his career before injuries caught up with him. He wore #84 and #87.

18. Safety/cornerback from Miami (1988-1996) who was taken 3rd overall by Detroit. He was a 1991 Pro Bowler and made 125 starts for the Lions, including every game in 5 of his 9 seasons. He had 12 interceptions for Detroit and was a key figure on the Lion teams that won the NFC Central in 1991 and 1993. He wore #36.

21. Undrafted quarterback from North Carolina State (1991-1993) who was mainly a back-up but did go 9-3 as a starter for those two NFC Central Champions. Plus he guided the team to its "most recent" post-season victory (24 ACROSS). He went on to the Bears (1994-1998) and played pretty well in 46 starts for some teams that were not very good. He wore #12.

22. Offensive tackle from Florida (1985-1995) who was a 1st round pick by Detroit and a 6-time Pro Bowler. He started 163 out of a possible 176 regular season games for the Lions and went on to play well for the Cardinals (1996-1998), Browns (1999) and Giants (2000-2001). He wore #75.

26. Wide-out from Virginia (1991-2001) who was a 1st round pick by Detroit and a 4-time Pro Bowler. A great leaper, he had 3 years with 100+ catches and is a member of the Lions Ring of Honor. He is #2 all-time for Detroit in catches (670), receiving yards (9,174) and touchdown catches (62). He wore #84.

27. Kicker from Washington State (1992-2012) who was a 2nd round pick and only played for Detroit. He was a 2-time Pro Bowler and his 495 field goals are the most in team history and #4 in NFL history. He holds the NFL records for most field goals of 40+ yards (189) and longest tenure with a single team (21seasons). He wore #4.

30. Linebacker from Georgia Tech (1993-1994) who had been a 3rd round pick by New Orleans (1986-1988), for whom he was a 4-time Pro Bowler.

He was a Pro Bowler for Detroit's 1993 Central Division winners and then finished with Oakland (1995-1997 and 1999). He had 107 career sacks and went on to serve in the Louisiana House of Representatives. He wore #56.

31. Defensive end from South Carolina State (1992-2004) who was a 1st round pick by Detroit and a 3-time Pro Bowler. He only played for the Lions and is 2nd all-time for the team with 95.5 sacks. He is behind only Alex Karras, who is credited with 100, which is odd because the NFL only began officially recognizing this statistical category in 1982. He wore #91.

33. Return specialist from Purdue (1989-1994) who had been a 2nd round pick by the Saints (1986-1988) and was a 4-time Pro Bowler for Detroit. He returned 5 kickoffs and 2 punts for touchdowns for the Lions and is the all-time franchise leader in career return yards on both kickoffs and punts. He wore #23.

34. Tight end from Iowa (2019-2021) who was a 1st round pick by Detroit and a 2020 Pro Bowler when he had 67 catches. He had 61 catches in 2021 but missed 5 games due to a thumb injury, which eventually required surgery in December 2021. He wears #88.

37. Amazing, 5'8", Hall of Fame running back from Oklahoma State (1989-1998) who had 1,100+ rushing yards in each of his 10 seasons and led the NFL in rushing yards 4 times. He wore #20.

42. Wide-out from USC (1994-2001) who was a 1st round pick by Detroit, for whom he had 4 seasons with 1,000+ receiving yards and 2 years with 80 catches. He is #3 all-time for the Lions in catches (469), receiving yards (6,499) and touchdown catches (35). He went on to a brief career in mixed martial arts in 2007. He wore #80.

44. The first name of the player referred to in 28 DOWN.

46. The first name of the player referred to in 19 ACROSS.

48. Detroit head coach (2009-2013) whose teams went 29-51, with a best record of 10-6 and a Wild Card berth in 2011. He was given this opportunity based on his success as a defensive coordinator for Tennessee (2001-2008). He went on to serve in the same capacity for Buffalo (2014) and Philadelphia, helping them win a Super Bowl in 2018.

49. The first name of the player referred to in 42 DOWN.

51. The first name of the player referred to in 12 DOWN.

53. Detroit head coach (1988-1986) who holds the franchise records for both most career wins AND losses by going 66-67 in the regular season. His teams made the playoffs 4 times and he was popular with his players and generally likable, which may explain how he escaped termination a number of times before the axe finally fell.

54. Quarterback from Georgia (2009-2020) who was taken 1st overall by Detroit and is the holder of all career passing records for the franchise. In 2022 he has the opportunity to lead his new team to the Super Bowl. He wore #9.

56. The 1995 team was blasted in the Wild Card Round by the _____ by a score of 58-37.

57. The 2011 team was beaten in the Wild Card Round by the _____ by a score of 45-28.

59. Heisman-winning running back from USC (2013-2014) who had been a 1st round pick by the Saints (2006-2010) for whom he was a 2010 Super Bowl Champion. He is the last man to rush for 1,000 yards in a season for Detroit (1,006 yards in 2013). He was a dynamic and versatile player with 477 career catches and 4 punt returns for scores. He wore #21.

60 Quarterback from Iowa (1986-1989 and 1991) who came in 2nd in Heisman balloting and was a 1st round pick by Detroit. He may be the most spectacular bust in the team's history of underachieving quarterbacks. He went 4-17 as a starter and was out of the NFL at age 28. He went on to fail as head coach at San Diego State (2006-2008). He wore #16.

61. The first name of the player referred to in 18 DOWN.

DETROIT LIONS

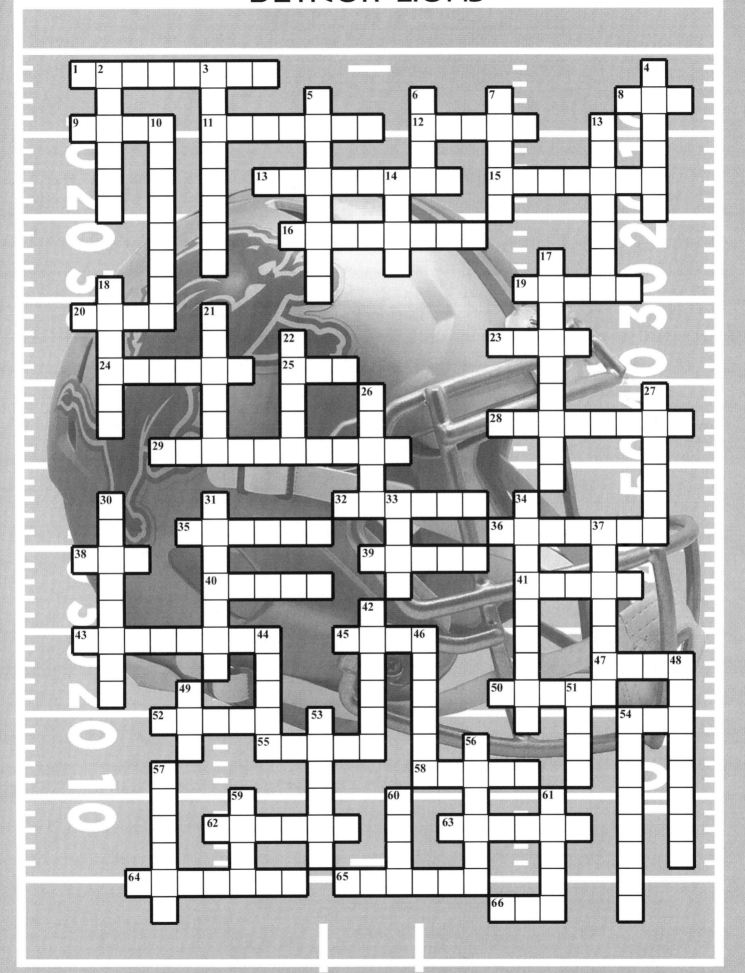

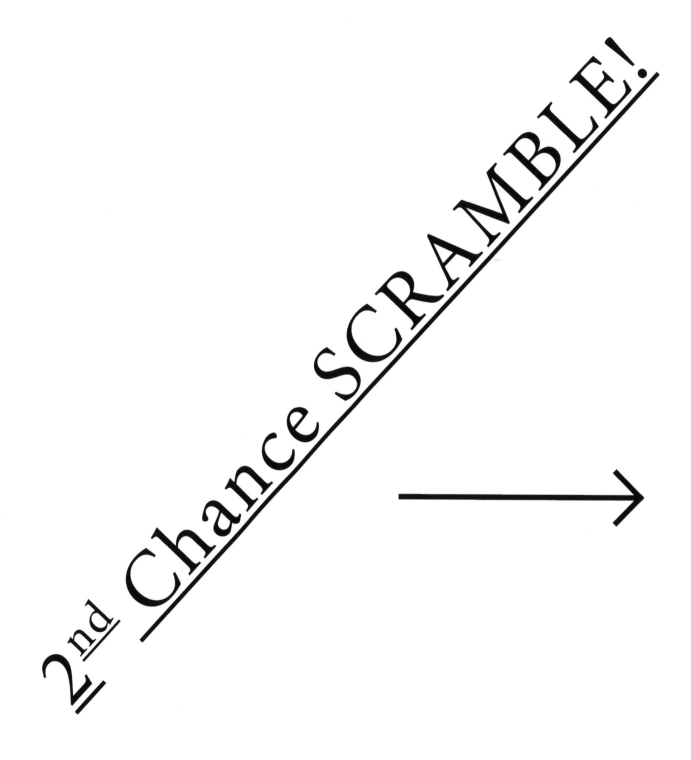

2nd Chance SCRAMBLE!

CXXXII

DETROIT LIONS

1. ALINPSEM ＿＿＿＿＿＿＿＿

8. JIM ＿＿＿

9. ANLG ＿＿＿＿

11. KICDIDR ＿＿＿＿＿＿＿

12. AAHNS ＿＿＿＿＿

13. LLLDECWA ＿＿＿＿＿＿＿＿

15. LLOEWRC ＿＿＿＿＿＿＿

16. AIATPCRI ＿＿＿＿＿＿＿＿

19. PEEET ＿＿＿＿＿

20. YLSA ＿＿＿＿

23. TEAT ＿＿＿＿

24. LLDASA ＿＿＿＿＿＿

25. ORY ＿＿＿

28. RPNRIAEM ＿＿＿＿＿＿＿＿

29. NHTIRRANOG ＿＿＿＿＿＿＿＿＿＿

32. IERGEG ＿＿＿＿＿＿

35. ORWHAD ＿＿＿＿＿＿

36. NONJHOS ＿＿＿＿＿＿＿

38. JIM ＿＿＿

39. AWNYE ＿＿＿＿＿

40. CCKHU ＿＿＿＿＿

41. IATNK ＿＿＿＿＿

43. ILMHLCTE ＿＿＿＿＿＿＿＿

45. YOBD ＿＿＿＿

47. SSRO ＿＿＿＿

50. SJONE ＿＿＿＿＿

52. PTAMA ＿＿＿＿＿

54. HSU ＿＿＿

55. ALNOS ＿＿＿＿＿

58. ASNUH ＿＿＿＿＿

62. YFURRE ＿＿＿＿＿＿

63. GLEORV ＿＿＿＿＿＿

64. PSTEHEN ＿＿＿＿＿＿＿

65. ROERGS ＿＿＿＿＿＿

66. YBL ＿＿＿

2. RTAPER ＿＿＿＿＿＿

3. CARMICUI ＿＿＿＿＿＿＿＿

4. PELHIP ＿＿＿＿＿＿

5. WLASILMI ＿＿＿＿＿＿＿＿

6. BALL ＿＿＿＿

7. BAHTC ＿＿＿＿＿

10. ALDOGAYL ＿＿＿＿＿＿＿＿

13. ETSWATR ＿＿＿＿＿＿＿

14. EKIR ＿＿＿＿

17. IEGEWTTPR ＿＿＿＿＿＿＿＿＿

18. EDSBLA ＿＿＿＿＿＿

21. RKAMRE ＿＿＿＿＿＿

22. NWROB ＿＿＿＿＿

26. OEROM ＿＿＿＿＿

27. AHSNNO ＿＿＿＿＿＿

30. IILNSGWL ＿＿＿＿＿＿＿＿

31. COPRERH ＿＿＿＿＿＿＿

33. RYAG ＿＿＿＿

34. SNNCEOOHK ＿＿＿＿＿＿＿＿＿

37. ENSSRAD ＿＿＿＿＿＿＿

42. TNMORO ＿＿＿＿＿＿

44. SLAOM ＿＿＿＿＿

46. DURSIA ＿＿＿＿＿＿

48. WHCATRZS ＿＿＿＿＿＿＿＿

49. PAT ＿＿＿

51. CRIE ＿＿＿＿

53. TSFNEO ＿＿＿＿＿＿

54. FAFDOTRS ＿＿＿＿＿＿＿＿

56. EGALES ＿＿＿＿＿＿

57. TNASIS ＿＿＿＿＿＿

59. BSUH ＿＿＿＿

60. ONGL ＿＿＿＿

61. ENKYN ＿＿＿＿＿

CXXXIII

ANSWER PAGE

Los Angeles Rams

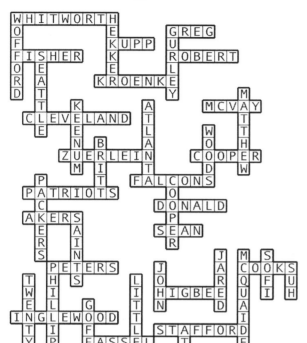

New Orleans Saints

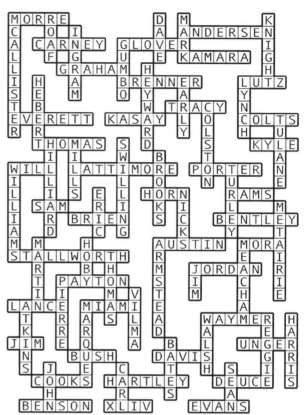

Carolina Panthers

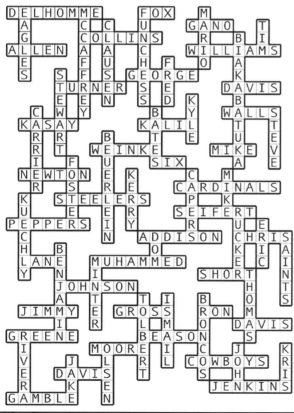

Arizona Cardinals

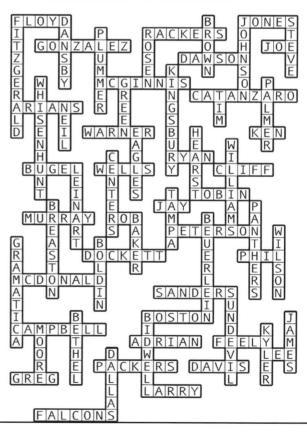

ANSWER PAGE

Dallas Cowboys

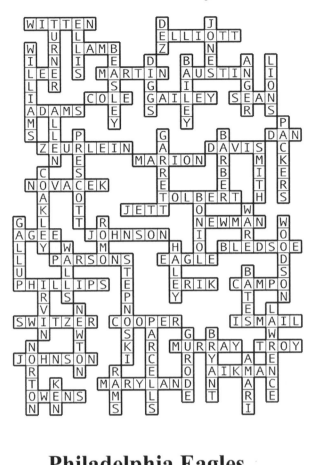

Washington Football Team

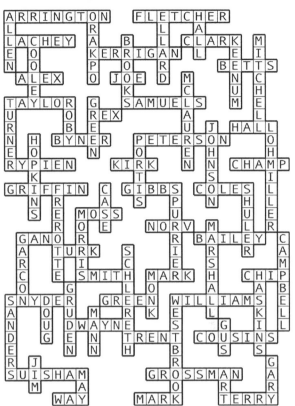

Philadelphia Eagles

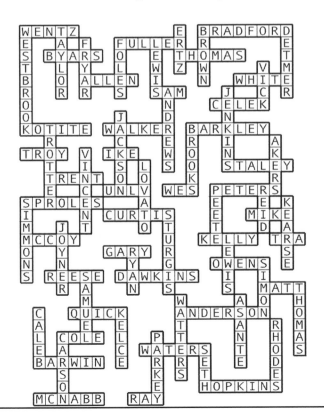

San Francisco 49ers

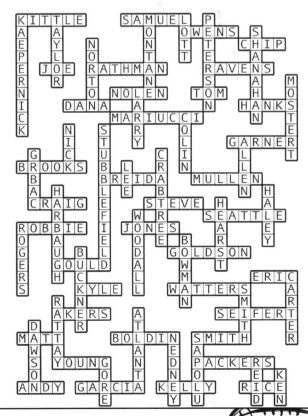

CXXXV

ANSWER PAGE

Minnesota Vikings

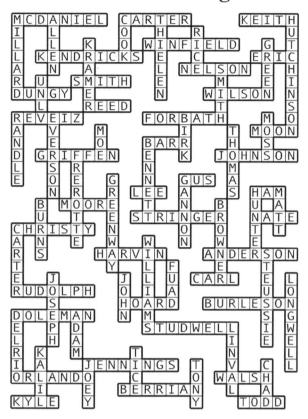

Tampa Buccaneers

Seattle Seahawks

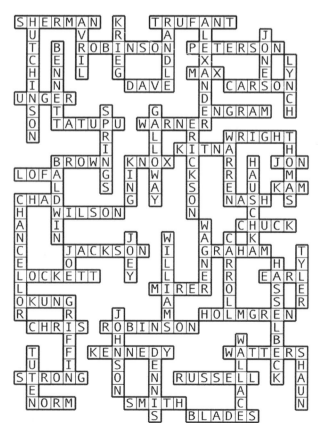

New York Giants

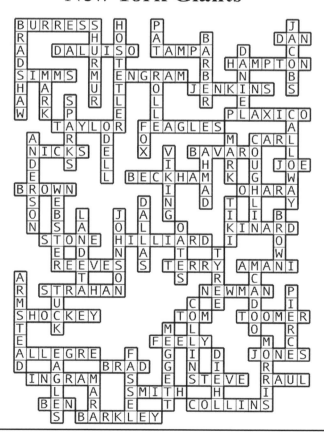

ANSWER PAGE

Green Bay Packers

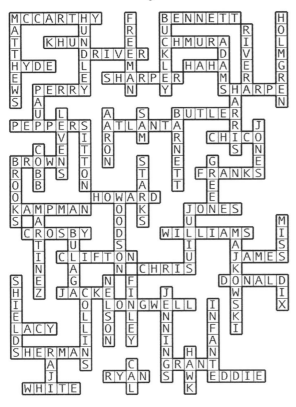

Chicago Bears

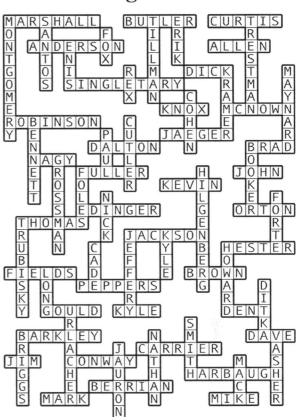

Atlanta Falcons

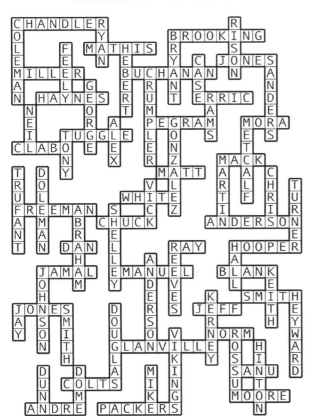

Detroit Lions

Made in the USA
Columbia, SC
01 April 2022

58301609R00076